I'm Gonna Win

by Andre J. Garant

I'm Gonna Win

Published by
Ewing Publications
P.O. Box 511
Somerset, MA 02726-05111

First Printing April 1999

Edited by Eric Rebello

Cover by David Aguiar (based on an idea by Andre J. Garant)

Author's photo by Grand Maison's Studio of Photography

ISBN: 0-7392-0210-3
Library of Congress Catalog Card Number: 99-94374

Printed in the USA by

MORRIS PUBLISHING
3212 East Highway 30 • Kearney, NE 68847 • 1-800-650-7888

Dedication

This book is dedicated to the oldest of my four nephews, Christophe C. Garant, age 11, of Philadelphia, PA. You are the greatest, Christophe! Although you don't possess all of the same characteristics as Matt "Basketball" Casey, you are the true meaning of a middle-grade adolescent who has inspired me to write this story. If I had one wish in the entire world, it would be that I could spend more time with you and your brothers. Then I would really get into some deep trouble. Be good, kiddo!

Acknowledgements

I would like to acknowledge all of my junior high students that I am currently teaching, or have taught, at St. Thomas More Church in Somerset, MA. To Meghan Ariagno, Bryan Botelho, Jessica Boulay, Kyle Bradbury, David Coulombe, Lindsay Dopart, Michael Fitzgerald, Adam Goncalo, Amanda Harrington, David Jameson, David Jones, Lynn Mello, Kevin Mullins, Christina Murray, Stephen Nadeau, John Niewola, Nadia Norman, Michael Perry, Niki Querim, Samuel Reidy, Brandon Silva, and last but certainly not least, Dean Toulan; all of you are the greatest. You have been a huge inspiration to me, and I thank you for your friendship, caring attitude, and dedication to learning. I will never forget any of you. Thanks for everything!

Also, special thanks to all of the junior high students at St. Thomas More Church that have actively participated in the Junior High Youth Ministry. All of you have made a huge difference in the lives of others. You should be congratulated for your hard work and constant dedication. Thank you!

A very special thank you goes out to Mr. Jason Kenney of the Somerset School Committee for the countless hours he spent typesetting this book into a camera-ready format, and also for doing all of the negotiating with Morris Publishing. The book would not be printed today if not for his tremendous involvement. Again, Jason, thanks for all of your help. Also, special thanks go out to Mr. Eric Rebello for acting as my official manuscript editor. Thanks for all of the late nights, Eric. Last but certainly not least, thank you to Linda Lafond of Somerset for her continual encouragement in getting me to publish this book. I'll see you in Dallas, Linda! Get ready for some serious dude ranching with Ray Krebbs.

1

Excitement

The flyer arrived in the mail on Friday. It said that the Senior League basketball tryouts would be held in less than two weeks. The moment I had been waiting for had finally arrived. Now that I was in sixth grade, I had once and for all earned the right to play on the Senior League, a team reserved for the highest grade at Clarkson Elementary School. And since I had always been one of the best basketball players in the history of Clarkson Elementary, my road to stardom would finally reach its peak in a matter of weeks. That's right, Matt "Basketball" Casey is about to become a world famous hero. I could see it right now, my name in bold print on the front page of the *Clarkson Observer*.

Uncle John keeps telling me to practice my shooting in the driveway, but I really don't need any practice. I'm great right now. If I weren't, then why would I be able to sink four three-pointers in a row while playing with him? Even he was a great basketball player back in his time. He told me so, and showed me some pictures of when he played at Lakeside Catholic Academy about forty years ago. Okay, I'm exaggerating a bit there. Uncle John is only thirty-nine years old, but that's still twenty-eight years older than I am. He's going to be my coach this year, and I'm really excited about that. You see, he has been coaching the Clarkson Elementary Senior League for the past three years, and now I get to be on his team. That's right. Matt "Basketball" Casey will be his star player, his hero, his Point Guard. You name it, I'll be it. Basketball has always been my life. I eat, sleep, and dream basketball. I don't even know why. I'm kind of short for my age and also a little on the skinny side. Most of my friends are taller than me, and there are even kids in the fourth and fifth grades that stand over me. But when it comes to shooting one on one, I can cream them all.

"Matthew, it's time for dinner," Mom said, calling up the stairs to me.

"Okay, Mom, I'm coming," I shouted back. "Matthew, where does she get that silly name from?" I whispered to myself, shaking my head. "It's Matt, or Basketball, but not Matthew." One thing I really hate is to be called Matthew. It just rubs me the wrong way. Even when I was still in diapers, I hated it. I don't know, it just sounds stupid, that's all. Matt sounds so much cooler, especially when you're eleven years old.

I bounded down the stairs, taking two steps at a time before crashing onto the floor in the foyer. "He lays one up. The crowd cheers him on, 'Go for the J, Matt, Go for the J' they shout at him. He swooshes one in, and the crowd responds by screaming, 'Yeah, Matt, you're so awesome.'"

"Matthew, honey, come on, please. Dinner is getting cold," Mom said from the kitchen. I frowned briefly before walking casually down the hall, the laces from my hi-tops swishing back and forth on the floor. I hate keeping them tied. I've never tripped on the laces

3

before, and besides, it looks so much cooler leaving them untied. Uncle John says it's bad for my ankles, but who really cares?

"What are we having for dinner tonight?" I asked casually.

"Roast turkey, mashed potatoes, stuffing, and steamed carrots."

"Sick, Mom. It's barely November and you're forcing the Thanksgiving thing on us already," I teased, shaking my head at Dad who was sitting at the end of the table. It's tough being an only child. It makes my job of keeping my parents in line that much harder.

"So, pal, tell me, how is school going?" Dad asked with a smile.

"It rots, as usual," I replied, flashing a mischievous grin in his direction.

"Matthew, honestly. That's not a nice thing to say," Mom said, taking her seat at the table.

"Well, it does. The only thing good about school this year is that I will get to play for Uncle John."

"You know, Matt, maybe that's not such a great thing," Dad said without looking up from his plate. "It may put him in an awkward situation having you on his team."

"What are you talking about, Dad? I *have* to be on his team. There's only one team for the sixth grade, and I certainly won't play on the fifth grade team again," I said, getting more serious now.

"I understand that, son, but you have to remember that he's not going to treat you any differently than any of the other kids on the team just because you're his nephew."

"I never said he would. Besides, I'm a great player, and that's all he cares about. He's going to be thrilled to have me on his team," I said with an air of confidence.

"Okay, kiddo, start on your dinner. We'll resume this conversation some other time," Dad said, frowning a little. What was he so worried about? Uncle John would be thrilled to have his nephew play for his team. That's right, Matt "Basketball" Casey would be the star of the

Clarkson Senior Team this year. I could already hear the crowd cheering wildly in my head.

2

My Best Pal

Perhaps I should tell you that David Jones is my best pal, my best friend in the whole wide world. That's right, David Jones from down on Hickory Street, the sixth grader who always wears a baseball cap, even when he goes to bed. He's really cool. We've been best pals now since we were three when his family moved in from Ohio. At first I thought David was kind of strange. He sucked his thumb until he was nearly eight and always whined if he didn't get his way. He's still pretty much of a big baby, but we get along like Mutt and Jeff. I'd be lost without him. This year is going to be so awesome. We're both trying out for my uncle's basketball team, and the neat thing about it is that we are both star players. Well, actually, I'm better than he is, but that's no secret since I'm better than *everybody*.

David plays a good Point Guard, just like me. I think it's because we're both a little on the short side. Neither one of us makes great Centers since we're not really tall enough to lay up the rebounds, but both of us are really good dribblers and ball passers. In fact, David has one of the meanest chest passes I've ever seen, while I can knock anybody down with my two-handed overhead passes. We're just a mean combination together, end of story.

I picked up the phone near my bed and dialed his number. Tryouts were already planned for next week and we needed to start talking about our positions on the team. We already knew both of us would make the pick hands down. That much was a given.

"Hey, David. What's up?" I asked.

"Hey, Matt. Not much. What's up with you?" David asked, sounding a little bummed out about something.

"Same stuff, different day," I informed him. "Tryouts are next Tuesday. Are you psyched, or what?"

"You bet I am. Your uncle better pick me. There's no way we can be on different teams. That would never work. Besides, we're both good enough to make the Senior Team."

"Don't worry, you're on. I'm going to talk to my uncle this weekend, and I'll sweet talk him real good. Just leave it to me, okay, pal?"

"Sure, dude. I want to be Point Guard," David said.

"No way. That's *my* position, David."

"Well, we'll just have to battle it out next week, won't we?"

"Yeah, right, like you'd really have a chance against me," I said, laughing a little. David was good, but not as good as the Mattster (that's me).

"Hey, Matt, we'll just have to see about it, won't we?"

"Yeah, whatever, David. I'm going to tell Uncle John to put you in as Off Guard. How's that for you?"

"No way, Matt," David blurted out. "We're both going to try for Point Guard, and whoever is better will get it."

"Yeah, sure. I just hope that we're the two best players on the team. Did you hear how many other sixth graders are trying out?"

"No, how many?" David asked.

"About forty or so, and there's only room for fifteen. Oh well, we've got nothing to worry about. It'll be us two and thirteen other average players," I said in a confident tone while smiling to myself.

"Now you're talking, dude. Listen, I have to go, but I'll see you tomorrow. Hey, how about some one on one this Saturday? My house. Be there or be square," David said.

"Yeah, sure, sounds good. See you in a while, crocodile."

"See ya later, alligator," David said, hanging up in my ear.

I smiled as I lay down on my bed and stared at the posters on the ceiling of my room. They were of Michael

Jordan and Kevin McHale. Basketball was so cool.
Whoever invented the sport should win a Nobel Prize or
something. Now there was a real person. Just think of
what he did for the youth of America. I was a basketball
freak who collected everything about the sport. I had four
pair of hi-top sneakers, a gazillion different basketball
jerseys and tank tops that I practiced in, and even about
twenty different pair of warm-up pants and sweatshirts
with all sorts of team emblems on them. Mom had even
bought me a red and blue warm-up suit with *Pistons*
spelled out all over it. They were my all-time favorite
team, next to the *Celtics*, that is. Not only do I have a
cool assortment of basketball clothing, but I also have
things like sheets, bedspreads, and bath towels with
basketball teams on them, not to mention my collection of
basketball caps and pennants to decorate my wall with. I
even have two pair of boxer shorts with basketball teams
on them. Way to go, Mattster!

Oh well, I guess you can understand by now how
much basketball means to me. But that doesn't mean that I

don't care for other sports. I also like soccer and baseball, but not nearly as much.

A knock sounded on my door. "Matthew, it's time to get ready for bed," Mom said from behind the door.

"Yeah, I know," I remarked without getting up. I glanced at my wristwatch. It was only 9:30. Hey, even my watch has basketballs on it. I almost forgot about that one, didn't I? I smiled as I thought about how great this year would be. Matt "Basketball" Casey would be the sixth grade hero, the all-time high scorer for Clarkson Elementary School. Of course, David would be runner-up. I couldn't forget about my best bud, now could I? Both of us were going to be basketball stars. In six years we would be hand picked by the NBA.

"Folks, it's Matt Casey, the all-time basketball great, and he's here today in person. He might be a little shorter than the others, but boy can he move around the court and sink those three pointers. That's right, everyone, Matt Casey, all the way from Clarkson, Indiana. What a bargain the NBA got when they found him..."

"Matthew, I don't want to have to tell you again. It's bedtime," Mom said from behind the door, louder now.

"Okay, already. I'm going. Gee whiz," I said, annoyed that she had interrupted my daydream. Oh well, there would be plenty of time for more of those. I was going to be a star, and nobody could stop me.

Andre J. Garant

3

Tryouts

"David, how do I look in this jersey?" I asked my best friend as we headed out of the locker room for basketball tryouts.

"Totally awesome, but not as cool as me," he answered, raising his hand for a high five. We were the dynamic duo. At last, Tuesday had arrived, and with it the chance to show off in front of our classmates at how good we were. We climbed up on the bleachers and took a seat in the top row.

"Hey, check out Ryan Wilson. He's probably got a good shot at making the team," David said casually, studying the other players who were strolling into the gym for tryouts.

"Yeah, maybe. Hey, look over there. It's Jason Nanz. He'll never get on the team. He needs to lose about fifty pounds first," I said before giggling out loud.

"I know. He can't play to save himself," David said, laughing with me.

From the side of the gym, Uncle John strolled out of the boys' locker room with a clipboard in his hand. He was followed by two other boys who pushed the ball carts out onto the gym floor. I smiled and waved at him.

"So, you're absolutely sure that your uncle said I had no problem at making Point Guard?" David asked, looking me straight in the eye.

"Yeah, um, he said so. But you have to impress him today," I stammered, knowing that I was lying to David. Uncle John hadn't said anything about choosing anyone yet. He told me that we would just have to wait until he saw all of the players on the court. Even after he watched all of us play for a full afternoon, he would still have to take several days before making a final decision as to who would make the team and who wouldn't.

Uncle John blew his whistle to get everyone's attention. "Quiet down, boys. As you probably all know, I'm John Casey, and I'm going to be the coach of the sixth grade team again this year. I'm glad to see such a great turnout for tryouts today. There are supposed to be thirty eight of you here, and only fifteen will be lucky enough to make the team. Those who don't may get drafted by the fifth grade team. Let me start off by taking a roll call of those who signed up."

I casually bit my nails as Uncle John called off the names of all the kids who were supposed to be here. David and I studied everyone who sat in the bleachers below us, laughing occasionally if we felt the kid was a geek or a nerd. This was going to be so much fun, showing all those amateurs that they didn't stand a chance against us two. Uncle John should have told us to stay home.

"Okay, we're only missing one person. At this time, I'd like everyone out on the floor. We're going to start off by practicing some basic drills."

With that said, I stood up and waited for David to take off his sweatshirt before we jumped down off the bleachers and jogged onto the court. The two of us grabbed a basketball off the rack and started dribbling around while practicing our foul shots.

"Hey, Matt and David. Put the balls back. We're not ready yet. I want everyone to sit down on the floor. We never start off until we have done our stretching exercises. These are very important for proper conditioning," Uncle John said, standing up in front of us.

"This is so stupid. Why can't we just play already? Nobody needs to stretch," I said to David, making a face at him.

"Yeah, really. This is for amateurs." We both laughed at each other.

"Boys, let's start off with some groin stretches. Put your sneakers together so that your knees are pointed out. Now grab each of your feet with your hands and bend forward until you feel it start to pull."

18

This was so retarded. I never stretched, and I could do this stuff without any pain whatsoever. Eleven-year-olds don't need to stretch. That's for older people.

After the exercises were over, Uncle John let us get up off the floor and pair up with a partner to begin some lane slides. David and I paired up together. When the whistle blew, we began the drill, each of us alternating as we continuously passed the ball back and forth to one another. After we had performed ten passes, we switched sides and began our way back to the other side where the other boys were waiting.

"Nice form, guys. Okay, next group," Uncle John called out, writing down some notes and watching the next two boys go at it.

"That was so easy, wasn't it?" I asked David, raising my hand for a high five.

"Sure was. Nice going, dude," David said, smacking me one.

The next drill was to practice our passing techniques. David and I paired up and performed a variety of chest passes, bounce passes, and overhead passes.

19

After we had done twenty passes without a single mistake, Uncle John blew his whistle.

"Great job, guys. Nice going."

"Yeah, we rule," I said loudly, smacking David another high five. The other boys were looking at us as if we were the best two players on the team. I bowed and smiled at them. That's right, I'm cool because I'm Matt "Basketball" Casey.

David and I waited until all the boys were done, all the while smiling and giggling as we cracked jokes about them.

"All right, boys. Now I want to see your dribbling techniques. We'll start off with some stationary dribbling, then we'll do some leg circles."

"This is way too easy," I said in a bored tone, my voice loud enough so that everyone could hear me.

"Excuse me, Matt. Is something wrong?" Uncle John asked me with a serious look on his face. By now, all seventy-four eyes from the other boys were glued to me.

"Um, no, Uncle John," I said, a little embarrassed. Some of the other boys started giggling, aware of the fact that the coach was my uncle.

"Well, then let's keep quiet," Uncle John warned. I grinned at David as he punched me in the arm, a huge smile on his face.

When our turn came, David and I ran out on the court and got into position. I was first up and began to dribble the ball around him. I moved in for the approach and faked him out, trying to dribble the ball between my legs.

Tweet! The whistle blew. "Whoa, stop for a minute, Matt. What are you doing? This is not a show off session. I don't want to see you trying to perform stunts like that again. Is that clear?" Uncle John asked.

"Yes, Coach. No problem," I said, trying not to laugh. The other boys were smiling and shaking their heads. Next, I began some whistle dribbling, changing direction as fast as I could while looking up at the basket. I had to admit, David was fast, so fast in fact that he was on top of me every second.

21

"Good footwork, Matt," Uncle John commented from the back of the court. When the whistle blew again, David began to dribble, and it was my turn to block him. He moved in close and performed a flawless leg circle, completely faking me out as he ran past me with the ball.

"Great fake out, David. Excellent job," Uncle John shouted. Some of the other kids began clapping. I did nothing more than crouch down and swear under my breath. I should never have let him by me like that. I took my position again and tried to block David as he approached me with another whistle dribble. Just when I thought he was going to my left side, he faked me out again and ran past me on my right side.

"Oh, shoot, David. You just faked me again," I yelled out, disappointed in my own judgment.

David stopped dribbling and smiled as the whistle blew.

Tweet Tweet! "Okay, guys. Great job. Next two up," Uncle John yelled, signaling that our session was over. David and I sat down in the corner and watched the other boys go at it. I had to be honest. They weren't all

22

that bad. Maybe I would have a *little* competition, but that's it. Once everyone had finished, the last practice drill was shooting techniques.

"All right, boys, last but not least I'd like to see your shooting abilities. David, Matt, and Jeff will start off. I want a combination of free throws and lay-ups. I also want at least one 'around the world.' Go ahead and dazzle me," Uncle John said, blowing the whistle and sending us out onto the court. I raced ahead of David and caught the throw from Jeff, dribbling defensively while maneuvering my feet with amazing skill. I faked David and went up for the free throw. *Swoosh*, the ball sounded as it sunk in for a three pointer.

"Excellent, Matt. Nice form, too," my uncle shouted. I couldn't help but form a huge smile. Next, Jeff grabbed the ball and began dribbling, using the whistle dribble technique. I hung on him like glue while David waited under the basket for the pass. Jeff tried to fake me out with a chest pass, but I intercepted the ball from him and began to lay up a jump shot. I sprung as high as I could in my Nike hi-tops and threw a flawless shot that sunk in for two points. *Swoosh!*

"Nice going, Matt," Uncle John called out. A round of applause came from the other boys. I was on fire now, and nothing could stop me. I jumped up for the rebound and faked David out, grabbing the ball away from his hands before dribbling back towards Jeff. "Okay, Matt, don't hog the ball now."

I ignored my uncle's request and began dribbling the ball forward, my eyes glued to the basket. Jeff came at me and tried to block me, but I pushed forward and knocked him to the floor while performing a flawless set shot which sunk in for another two. The whistle blew with a shrill. *Tweeeet!*

"Matt, what was that?" Uncle John yelled, jogging onto the court. I looked down at Jeff who lay sprawled on the floor.

"Matt, what did you do that for?" David asked, arriving at my side and kneeling down to help Jeff up from the floor.

"Sorry, Jeff," I muttered as Uncle John arrived to check on his condition. After making sure that Jeff wasn't hurt, he looked me straight in the eye.

"Matt, I don't know what that was all about, but it goes totally against everything I've taught you. I specifically asked you not to hog the ball. And why did you pummel Jeff like that? That was a definite foul."

"But I got it in, didn't I?" I asked, getting a little upset that nobody had said "Nice shot" or "Way to go, Matt." Nobody even gave me a pat on the back.

"That's not the point here," Uncle John said, giving me a look of disappointment. "Okay, next group up. You guys have a seat. I've seen enough."

The three of us sauntered back to the sidelines and sat down on the floor.

"Matt, you should have passed it to me. I was wide open," David said.

"Yeah, but I had a clear shot, and I knew I could make it."

"So what? Coach doesn't care about that. He's grading us on our ability to follow the rules and be good sports. He doesn't like it when you hog the ball like that. We all know you're a great player already."

I frowned and stared down at the floor. "You're probably right," I said, shrugging my shoulders. "Well, that's it for today. We're done, and I hope he liked what he saw."

"Me too," David said, turning his head away to watch the other boys on the court. He was not happy with me.

After the last boys had taken a shot at the shooting drills, Coach blew his whistle and indicated for all of us to sit down.

"All right, boys. Each one of you did a fantastic job today. I will be making my decision during the next week about who the fifteen boys will be. Those of you who are lucky enough to be picked will be a member of the Clarkson Challengers, and each of you will get your own uniform. We will be going with the traditional green shorts and white tank tops with matching warm ups. I will call the fifteen players next Tuesday, exactly one week from today. Thanks for coming this afternoon. You'd better get changed quickly since the buses are already here."

I stood up and grabbed David's arm. "I just know we're going to get picked. I can feel it," I said, smiling at David as we began walking back to the locker room.

"Matt, can I see you for a minute?" Uncle John asked, motioning for me to come over to him.

"Yeah, sure," I said before patting David on the back and running over to greet my uncle with a smile from ear to ear.

"Have a seat, pal," he said to me, patting the wooden bench with his hand. I sat down next to him and waited to hear the good news. I know, he's going to tell me now that I'm going to get Point Guard. That way I won't have to lose any sleep over it this week.

"Matt, I think I should let you know that I am going to consider you just like any of the other boys who tried out today. The fact that you're my nephew does not mean I'm going to favor you over any of the others." My smile faded to a look of confusion. "I didn't appreciate the stunts you were pulling out there. I know you're a good player, but you have to remember that there are other good players, too. You tried to make a show off of yourself today, and I don't like that."

"What do you mean, a show off?" I asked, beginning to get a little hot under the collar.

"Come on, Matt. I've known you since the day you were born. You're a great kid, a great nephew, and I love you to death. But you have to stop thinking that you're great all the time. A true winner doesn't act selfish like that. Please, tone down on the showing off and you'll do just fine. You don't need to impress me. I already know you're an excellent player."

"Uncle John, I'm not showing off for anyone," I said, trying to defend myself. The last thing I needed right now was having him tell me how to act on the court. "You *have* to pick me if you want your team to be the best, simple as that."

"See, that's what I mean, kiddo. There you go again. It's not always about winning, Matt. Look, we'll talk about this some other time. You better go and get changed up or you'll miss the bus." He gave me a friendly pat on the back to send me off.

"But, Uncle John, you *are* going to pick me, aren't you?" I asked, not satisfied one bit with what I had just heard.

He shook his head briefly. "Matt, I already told you. I need the full week to think about it. I'll talk to you later."

I pursed my lips and thought about arguing with him. How could he say that he needed to think about it? He had the best eleven-year-old right in front of him and he needed to *think* about it? This was totally ridiculous. I got up and ran across the gym to the locker room. By the time I ran in the door, David was already coming out, his gym bag slung over his shoulder.

"So, are we on the team, or what?" he asked, sticking his arm out to stop me.

"Don't even ask," I said, shaking my head. "Look, you better go. I'll see you tomorrow."

"Okay, see ya, buddy," David said, smiling at me. I tried to smile back, but the best I could do was nod my head before walking into the locker room. This was great, just great. The first day of tryouts and my uncle was already upset with me. The only thing I could do now was go home and put on my whining act to convince Dad to call Uncle John and get him to pick me for the team. Maybe it would work. I had nothing to lose at this point. I had to get picked for the Challengers. I just *had* to.

Torture Sets In

At the dinner table later that night, I couldn't help but push the food around on my plate as if it were pure poison, and meatloaf was one of my favorite meals.

"Matt, what's wrong? You seem to be down in the dumps about something. Did the tryouts go okay today?" Dad asked.

I shrugged my shoulders. "I guess. I don't know," I answered without enthusiasm.

"Well, what do you mean by that? Obviously something is bothering you."

"Dad, I'm fine, really. It's nothing," I said, trying to put up a good front so that he wouldn't know what had happened this afternoon with Uncle John. The more I thought about asking him to call Uncle John, the worse I felt. On the one hand, I didn't want either of them to think I was a baby, but on the other hand I wanted to make the team so badly that it was literally torturing me to death. Making that team meant the whole world to me right now. Just a few days ago, I was totally sure that I would not only make the team, but that I would be Point Guard. Now, I was beginning to feel unsure of anything, and wondered whether Uncle John really meant what he said about me acting like a show off.

Later on, Dad walked into my room and sat down on my bed. I was listening to the latest album by *Fishbone*, my favorite rock group.

"Hey, kiddo. Can I talk to you for a minute?"

I shut off my Discman and sat up on the bed. "Yeah, sure, Dad."

"Listen, I know Matt Casey quite well. In fact, I've known him for eleven years and seven months, and I can usually tell when there is something bothering him."

"Okay, Dad," I said, finally giving in to him. Besides, what good would it do to hold my frustration inside? "You *really* want to know what happened today?"

"Yes, Matt, I do. I want to hear everything about how your practice went, the whole nine yards, the whole kit and caboodle, the whole ball of..."

"Dad," I said, giving him a friendly punch in the arm. "I get the picture already. Everything went fine except for a few silly mistakes I made on the court. But when practice was over, Uncle John called me over and told me that he wasn't going to treat me any differently because I was his nephew."

"Yes, well that's good. Did you think he *would* treat you any differently?" Dad asked with a curious grin.

I frowned and turned my head away. Did he want me to tell him the truth? "I don't know. I guess so, in a way."

"But, Matt, we already discussed that a few weeks ago. Uncle John has a responsibility as a coach. He can't favor any kids more than some others. He has a duty as the coach to treat everyone the same, regardless of whether he knows some of them, or likes some of them more because they may be a better player. Please don't put him in a difficult situation. I'm sure this is tough enough for him as it is."

"Yeah, fine, Dad, but I'm clearly better than all of those kids, even David. It's obvious. Half of them can't even sink a basket." I was beginning to get worked up now. How could he take Uncle John's side on this?

"Listen, Matt. We both know that you're probably better than a lot of those kids, and I'm also sure that Uncle John knows that, too. He's not going to shortchange you when he makes his pick. If you did a good job out there today, then you have nothing to worry about," Dad said, smiling as he placed a hand on my shoulder.

"I guess, but he told me that I have to stop acting like a show off. He said that winners don't act selfish on the court."

"Well, were you acting like a show off out there today?" Dad asked, the smile gone from his face.

"No," I said, defending myself. "But I think Uncle John got mad at me when I didn't pass the ball to David during the shooting drills. I knew I could make the shot by myself, so I laid it up and sunk it in, but not before I knocked Jeff Aldrich down on the floor."

"Oh, Matt," Dad said with a disappointed tone. "You didn't knock him over on purpose, did you?"

"Of course not, Dad," I lied. "But it seemed like everyone got mad at me because I didn't pass the ball to David. I mean, he was wide open and all, but I wanted to sink it on my own."

Dad took a deep breath and stared at my pennants on the far wall.

"Dad," I said in a low whisper.

He looked over at me. "Yes, Matthew."

"Do you think you could call Uncle John and talk to him for me?" I asked, my eyes staring up at him with a hopeful gaze.

"What for?"

"I don't know. Maybe you could tell him that I would be a good Point Guard on the team. Or, maybe you could find out if he knows already what position I'll play. Just talk to him, please. Pretty please, Dad," I said, my voice beginning to take on that whine that I had mastered to a science by the age of six.

"Matthew, please don't act like this right now. I am not going to call him to do that. You know that's wrong," Dad answered firmly.

"Why, Dad?" I asked, my voice getting higher and louder.

"Because it's not fair to the other players, that's why. You know that. I know you do. Come on, stop acting like a little kid."

"So you won't do it?" I blurted out, now getting mad.

"Matt, no, I won't do it. Listen, let's end this discussion right now. Do yourself a favor and relax. Uncle John will make his decision this week, and I honestly feel that he'll pick you. Don't worry about it so much."

"How can you say that?" I shouted out, the blood beginning to boil in my veins. "Basketball is my life. I love it. I *have* to be on that team, and I *have* to be Point Guard." Dad gave me a surprised look as I stared at him with an angry face. It was clear that he, my own father, was not going to help me out here.

"Matt, I think you should get ready for bed," Dad said, getting up from my bed and walking to the door.

"Thanks for *nothing,* Dad," I yelled out, slamming my fist into my pillow with all my might.

Andre J. Garant

5

The Verdict

By the time next Tuesday rolled around, I had practically made myself sick wondering whether or not I would be the new Point Guard for the Clarkson Challengers. David and I had even argued with one another, figuring we both had an equal shot at the position. After the schoolbus dropped me off on the corner, I ran home as fast as I could, my toes digging into my Nike hi-tops as I sprinted down the street. I bounded through the back door and dropped my bookbag on the floor with a thud.

"Mom, did Uncle John call yet?" I asked while trying to catch my breath.

"No, sweetheart, not yet. I have a treat for you today. Sit down and have a piece of my coconut custard pie. It's left over from my lunch with..."

"Thanks, Mom," I said, grabbing the piece of pie with my hands and inhaling it as I ran up the stairs to my room, crumbs dropping everywhere.

"Matthew, come back here right now. Where are your manners?" she yelled.

"I can't. I have to call David," I shouted back before shutting my bedroom door and kicking off my hi-tops. *Clunk, clink* they sounded as they bounced off my desk. After finishing the pie and wiping my hands on my jeans, I dove headfirst on my bed and grabbed my portable phone to call David. Perhaps he had found out already.

"Hello," David said happily from the other end of the line.

"Hey, dude. Did Coach call you yet?" I asked.

"No, but I told you I would call you as soon as I find out. Listen, you're tying up the line. I'll talk to you later," David said before hanging up in my ear.

"Sure, whatever," I muttered, rolling over to turn on my stereo and blasting *Everclear* until the walls of my bedroom began to shake. As I listened to the stereo, I watched the minutes on my watch tick on by. Soon it got dark out, and it was time for dinner. Still no call from Coach or from David. Uh oh, this was not good.

After eating a quick dinner of pork chops, lima beans (*yuk*), and wild rice, I sauntered into the family room to catch the tail end of the sports on the news.

"So, no call yet?" Dad asked me as he flipped through the newspaper.

I shook my head. "Nope."

"Well, keep your chin up, pal. It's early yet," he said, trying to keep me on the optimistic side of things. I plopped down on the couch and watched the news until it was over. Then the repeats of *Seinfeld* came on, followed by *Home Improvement*. It was almost 8:00, and I still hadn't received a phone call. Finally, I got up and moped over to where Mom and Dad were sitting at the kitchen table, paying bills.

"I can't believe this. He should have called by now," I said miserably.

Before anyone could say anything, the phone rang, jolting me dead in my tracks. I looked at Dad, who looked at me.

"Well, pick it up, kiddo. It's probably for you," he said with a smile.

I ran over to the phone and picked it up. "Hello."

"Hey, Matt. Sorry I couldn't call sooner, but my Dad was on the phone since 6:30 talking long distance with one of his business partners, and we were having dinner before that. So, did he call you yet?" David asked, his voice brimming with excitement.

"No, how about you?" I asked.

"Yeah, around 5:15. Guess what, dude?"

I hesitated on the line, not knowing if I wanted to hear what David was about to say. He better not have gotten Point Guard. And why hadn't Uncle John called *me* yet? I mean, 5:15 was nearly three hours ago.

"Hey, Matt, are you there, buddy?"

"Yeah, I'm here, David," I answered softly.

42

"I'm the new Point Guard for the Clarkson Challengers," David shouted out, practically making me deaf on the phone.

What? Did I just hear him correctly? "Wait a minute. *You* are going to be Point Guard?" I asked, still not quite believing what he had just told me.

"Yup, that's right, pal. Say, how come you didn't get a call yet? Are you sure you're not pulling my leg?" David asked, practically giggling with excitement.

"*No*, David, I did not get a stupid call yet," I shouted into the phone, now getting angry and worried at the same time. How come I didn't get a phone call from Uncle John? "Listen, I'll talk to you tomorrow," I said sharply before hanging up the phone.

"So, what did David have to say?" Dad asked, now standing up and walking over to me.

I looked down at the floor and tried to hold back the few tears that began to well up in my eyes. "Just forget it," was all I could say with a shaky voice.

43

Dad came over to my side and put his arm around my shoulder. "Matt, I'm sure you'll be getting your phone call soon."

I finally looked up and locked eyes with my father. "You don't understand, Dad. Uncle John called David almost three hours ago. Why hasn't he called *me*?" I asked sadly. "David got Point Guard, too. What does that leave me?"

Before Dad had a chance to comfort me, I squirmed free from his grip and ran out of the kitchen and up the stairs to my room. I slammed the bedroom door as hard as I could and jumped onto my bed. If I was going to cry, then I sure didn't need anybody seeing me. After I had pounded my fists into my comforter and cried for a solid ten minutes, the front doorbell rang. I picked my head up and listened intently. I could hear Dad and Mom talking and laughing from downstairs. Suddenly, the sound of footsteps got closer from the hallway followed by a knocking on my door.

"Matt, may I come in?" It was the voice of Uncle John.

I jumped up and ran to open the door. "Hi, yeah, come on in," I said happily, flashing a smile from ear to ear at my uncle.

"I'm really sorry that it took me so long to get to you. I was going to call you, but I figured it would be better if I came over to see you in person." Uncle John and I sat down on my bed.

"I heard that David got Point Guard," I said sadly, wanting him to know that I wasn't happy about that.

"Well, yeah, that's right, Matt. But I did some serious thinking this past week, and I want you to be my Off Guard. What do you think of that?" Uncle John asked, his eyes lit up like a Christmas tree.

I formed a weak smile. "Off Guard, Uncle John? But I wanted Point Guard. Don't you think I'm better than playing silly Off Guard? That's a good position for someone like Todd Anderson or Billy Graham." I shook my head and looked down at my feet. Off Guard. That was a stupid position. It was the last thing I wanted on the team.

"Matt, aren't you happy? I thought you'd like Off Guard. It's a great position for you. I couldn't make you Center because you're a little too short for that and..."

"Off Guard *sucks*," I shouted out, standing up and walking over to my closet, keeping my back turned to Uncle John. I picked up my nerf basketball and threw it at the wall as hard as I could.

"Matt, come on. Let's act civilized about this. Off Guard is a highly respected position."

I swung my head around to face my uncle. "It's a *stupid* position," I yelled at the top of my voice. "If you keep me there, then I quit the team. I want to be Point Guard or nothing at all." I was so mad that my arms and legs were shaking with adrenaline and my face was getting hot.

Uncle John gave me a confused look, then got up and made his way to my bedroom door. "I'm sorry you feel that way, Matt."

He then left the room, leaving me madder than ever. I hated him. He was the worst uncle anybody could ever have. I was his nephew, the best player on the team, and all he could do for me was to put me in as stupid Off Guard? I hated him more than anybody right now. He could take his stupid team and stick it where the sun didn't shine. Let them lose every game of the season for all I cared. Without me, they didn't stand a chance of taking the championship.

Andre J. Garant

I'm Sorry

The next night at the dinner table, Mom and Dad decided to have a little talk to set me straight.

"Matt, you should be ashamed of the way you acted in front of your uncle. I demand that you call him after dinner and apologize to him. I don't know how you could have acted so foolishly. What on earth were you thinking?" Dad asked, staring at me with an upset look.

I pushed the peas and carrots around on my plate without looking up. I was too ashamed to look him in the eye. He was right. I had been a complete jerk to yell at Uncle John the way I did last night, even if he didn't give me Point Guard.

"Matthew Derrick Casey, did you hear what I just said?" Dad asked, now sounding angry.

"Yes, I did, Dad. I'll call him after dinner," I answered softly.

"And I want you to promise me that you will never act like that again. If you do something like that once more, I will take you off the team and ground you for the entire season. I don't think you'd like having to come home every afternoon and work on your homework until dinner, but that's what I'll do if you don't shape up real soon."

"I got it, Dad," I said in a low mumble, finally glancing up to look him in the eye. The rest of dinner was miserable, to say the very least. The truth was I felt horrible about yelling at my uncle the way I did last night. I don't know what happened to me. It was almost as if something just snapped in my head. Yeah, I wanted Point Guard more than anything else, but Off Guard wasn't such a bad position. I mean, it was the next best position on the team. It was an alternate to Point Guard, and was a spot reserved for the team's best long-range shooter, which of course was me. Besides, Off Guard was known as a spot for the second best dribbler on the team, too. Maybe I could work things out after all.

After dinner was over, I went upstairs to my room to call Uncle John. It was one of those conversations that required a little privacy, and the last thing I wanted was Mom and Dad to listen in on me. I picked up the phone and dialed his number. He answered on the second ring.

"Hi, Uncle John. It's me, Matt."

There was a second or two of silence. "Yeah, hi, Matt. How are you?"

"Um, I'm okay, and you?" I asked, trying to be as polite as possible.

"Well, I guess I'm not too bad, especially considering I lost a team member for the Challengers, not to mention my favorite nephew."

Sure, rub it in, Uncle John. I felt bad enough as it was. "Well, that's why I'm calling you. I, um, wanted to just say that I was sorry for acting like a jerk last night. I didn't mean what I said." The words came out painfully slow, almost as if someone were holding a gun to my head. Apologizing was never one of my strong points.

"Matt, I'm glad to hear that. I know you didn't mean what you said. Do you think you'd still like to be on the team?" Uncle John asked, sounding hopeful.

"Yeah, if you'll let me and all. I mean, will you take me back, as Off Guard?"

"I'd be honored to have you back on the team. I didn't know what I was going to tell the other boys about you. Listen, thanks for calling, Matt. Can you make our first practice on Saturday morning at 10:00?" he asked.

"Uncle John, I'll definitely be there. Thanks," I said happily, now feeling like I had just dropped a load of bricks off my back. After hanging up, I was so happy that I blasted my stereo and danced around my room, throwing my nerf basketball through the hoop on my bedroom door at the same time. This was going to be so great. Matt "Basketball" Casey was back in action. That's right, folks, he's back, so move aside.

7

Practice

It was Saturday morning, the first day of practice. I was rummaging through my basketball clothes, trying to figure out what I should wear. I wanted to look cool, yet fashionable. I was a little strange about clothes sometimes. Mom often yelled at me for not caring about how I looked in school, but when it came to basketball practice with my friends, I always had to look my best. After all, my middle name wasn't "Basketball" for nothing. Well, that's not my real middle name. My real middle name is Derrick, but "Basketball" sounds so much cooler. There's no comparison.

"Matt, are you ready yet?" Dad shouted up the stairs to me.

"Just a second, Dad. I haven't decided what sneakers to wear."

"Come on, Matt. You'll be late."

"Cool your jets, already," I mumbled under my breath as I pulled on my newest pair of hi-tops which went pretty well with my red and blue warm up suit. Underneath, I had on a pair of black mesh shorts and a tank top.

At the school, I met up with David right away. He was shooting some baskets in the far end of the gym.

"Hey, dude, what's up?" I asked as I ran over to join him.

David threw the basketball to me. "Hey, Mattster. Not much, buddy." We exchanged a friendly high five before shooting some baskets. Once all of the other boys had arrived, Uncle John blew his whistle. *Tweet Tweet!*

"Okay, guys. Come over here and sit down on the floor. I have some things to go over with you before we begin practice." All of us gathered on the floor in front of him. "I'd like to introduce the members of the team. Most of you know each other already, but this is just in case you don't. Of course, there are fifteen of you on the Challengers this year. The starting lineup includes David Jones as Point Guard, Jesse Barrett as Small Forward, Matt Casey as Off Guard, Christopher Medeiros as Big Forward, and Jason Standish as Center." There was some clapping and whistling from the others. I reached over and gave David a burning high five. "At this time, I'd like to tell you what your uniform numbers will be. You will pick them up right after practice today."

"I want number 7. That's always my lucky number," I whispered to David.

"Listen up. The numbers are: Jones, 9, Barrett, 5, Casey, 13, Medeiros, 7, Standish, 11, Copley, 4, Dailey, 3, McDonald, 8, Sullivan, 15, Walker, 12, Graham, 16, Raposo, 21, Walsh, 19, Gray, 10, and Ortiz, 14." There was a tremendous amount of whispering and smiling after Coach announced the numbers.

"I got 13. That rots! Doesn't he realize that 13 is bad luck?" I asked, making a face at David.

"He should. Stinks for you, pal. I got 9, my second favorite number."

"Yeah, and stupid Chris Medeiros gets number 7. He doesn't deserve it, nor does he deserve to play Big Forward. He stinks at this game. What a joke..."

"Matt, I'm talking right now. When I talk, you listen. Understand?" Uncle John asked, giving me a stern look.

I shook my head. "Yeah, whatever you say." The words had slipped out of my mouth rather bitterly, and Uncle John quickly picked up on it.

"Matt, perhaps you'd like to sit the practice out on the bleachers."

"No, what did I do?" I asked defensively, giving him an innocent look. The other boys were completely silent.

"I don't like your attitude today, Matt."

"Well, if you hadn't given me number 13. What a stupid number, plus it means bad luck." I then shook my head and rolled my eyes.

"Matt, go sit in the bleachers. I don't have time for this today."

"What did I do?" I yelled out, remaining seated on the floor.

"Matt, please don't give me a hard time today," Uncle John said in a tired voice.

"You're a jerk," was all I said as I sprung to my feet and walked slowly over to the bleachers. The blood was boiling through my veins, and I actually wanted to walk up to my uncle and let him have one. Who was he to pick on me when I didn't even do anything wrong? He could go you know where. There was a long period of silence, only mixed in with a few whisperings and giggles from the other boys on the team. I think that Uncle John was in shock from what I said to him.

"This sucks, big time," I muttered under my breath as I sat down on the top bleacher and watched the other boys on the team get up and start going through the various drills. Once Uncle John had gotten them started, he walked over in my direction. When I saw him climbing the bleachers, heading directly for me, I turned my face away and pretended to read the pennants hanging on the far wall.

He sat down beside me. "Matt, what is it, buddy? You haven't been acting yourself lately."

"Uncle John, just leave me alone."

He put his hand on my shoulder to get my attention. "I will not leave you alone. Something is wrong with you and I want to know what it is."

"You want to know what's wrong with me?" I shouted out, my voice echoing throughout the gym so loud that the other players stopped practicing. "I'll tell you what's wrong. First, you pick David to be Point Guard. I should have gotten that position. I'm better than him by a mile. Second, you make Chris Medeiros Big Forward. He doesn't even know his thumb from his butt. Then, you give me stupid number 13, which I'm sure you know is a bad luck number. Do you want me on this team or not?" I yelled, holding everyone's attention. I stared into my uncle's eyes.

"Matt, lower your voice this instant. I will not tolerate this type of behavior from any member of my team. I don't understand you..."

"Because you don't give a darn about me, that's why." By now, my face was scarlet red and I knew that my temper had gone over the edge. It had happened without me even trying to do it. The last time this happened to me was back in the fourth grade nearly two years ago when Kevin Mills stole my drawing in art class and hung it up in the girls' locker room for everyone to see. I nearly killed him I was so mad. It scared me when I got angry like this since I clenched my fists and looked for the nearest object in sight that I could punch. Dr. Liebowitz, the school psychologist, said a few years ago that I had some sort of mental disorder that made me snap every once in a while. It didn't happen often, but let me tell you, when it did, I was not a pretty sight to look at. I once lost it in front of Mom back when I was seven and bit her arm so badly that she had to have stitches put in where my teeth had punctured her skin. She still has scars there to this day.

"Matthew, I don't have time or patience for your behavior today. If you can't control yourself then I will have no choice but to suspend you from the team," Uncle John said, getting irritated himself.

That's when it finally happened. The straw had broken the camel's back. I stood up and kicked him square in the chest with my right sneaker, knocking over his clipboard. He grabbed my foot with his hand and held it so that I lost my balance and fell down on the bleachers. By now, stars were forming in my eyes, and the final switch went off in my mind. It said for me to attack and kill the predator. I got up and lunged forward, quickly swinging my right arm as hard as I could. *Smack,* came the sound of my arm clocking Uncle John's head. His glasses fell off his face, through the bleachers, and onto the floor below. I swung again, harder this time, catching his nose with a direct hit that made him double over in pain.

"Matt, what are you doing? Please stop," Uncle John yelled.

My mind told me to continue the attack. I kicked him once again in the chest as hard as I could, my legs moving with incredible speed as I pummeled his ribs with a barrage of direct hits.

"Matt, cut it out," David yelled, now running up the bleachers to stop me.

"Shut up," I shouted, turning to face him as he arrived at my side. He stopped, but only for a brief second before grabbing both my arms and holding them back. I struggled to break free so I could continue my attack on Uncle John, but Chris and Jason had now arrived to help David.

"Hold him back, Chris," Jason said as they pulled me away from my uncle.

"Let me go," I shouted, my eyes focused on one thing; that of beating my own uncle to a pulp. I would show him who was boss here.

"Matt, you've gone bonkers on us," David shouted, stretching my arms back to the point where they were about to rip out of their sockets. "Calm down, already."

Suddenly, a calming effect took hold of me and I relaxed in David's arms to the point where I collapsed onto the bleachers, my body taking on the form of a wet noodle.

"Jason, hold him now. Don't let him go," Chris said as they slowly lowered me down onto the bleachers where I lay motionless, my eyes now glazed over as I stared up at the lights on the ceiling. A dizzy sensation spread up through my spine causing a tingling in my arms and legs. That's when I fainted.

What's My Problem

My eyes opened slowly, heavy from a deep sleep. I looked around, studying the surroundings of the room. I had never been here before. There were all sorts of medical devices, carts, and tools spread around the room. When I looked down at myself, I realized that I was in a hospital bed, wearing some kind of robe that was tied behind my back. My bare feet were sticking out the bottom.

"Charles, come quick. He woke up." It was Mom's voice, and I smiled as I saw her come through the door. She stood beside me and kissed my forehead.

"Mom, what's going on here? Where am I?" I asked, totally confused.

"Shh, sweetheart. You're at the hospital, that's all. You had a little accident at basketball practice this morning, but don't be alarmed. You're going to be just fine."

Dad came walking in the room and also bent over to kiss me. My mouth was as dry as a piece of wood. I tugged at the IV line stuck in my right arm.

"Matthew, leave that alone. Here, give me your hand," Mom said, grabbing my hand so that I wouldn't disturb the IV solution as it dribbled down the plastic tube and into my arm.

"What the heck is going on here? Why am I in the hospital?" I demanded.

"Matt, just relax, pal. Nothing's wrong with you. Do you remember what happened at basketball practice this morning?" Dad asked, smiling down at me.

I thought hard. "No, not really." But then a light bulb went on in my head. The more I thought about it, the more that came back to my memory. Suddenly, it was all clear to me. The kicking, punching, yelling, *all* of it. I made a sour face and looked up at Dad.

"What's up, pal? Do you want to say something?" he inquired, grabbing my left hand and squeezing it.

"Um, I don't know what happened with me, but I remember yelling at Uncle John. I was real mad at him for some reason." I knew exactly why I was mad at him, but I didn't want to reveal everything to Mom and Dad. I felt bad enough as it was.

"Honey, what happened between you two? He told us that you..."

"Shh, Marge, let's give him a chance to speak on his own," Dad said, interrupting her. Both of them looked down at me and waited to hear my side of the story.

"I need to go to the bathroom," was all I said, squeezing my legs together as I felt my bladder ready to burst.

Dad reached for a container that was kept under the bed and handed it to me. "Here, can you go in this? I don't know where the nurse is and you're hooked up to that IV right now."

"I'm not going in *that* thing," I shrieked, looking at him as if he were crazy. I wasn't an old invalid who had

65

to go in a cardboard container. I was eleven years old, for God sakes. "I want to use the bathroom," I stated firmly.

"Matt, we'll leave the room while you do your business," Dad said, leaving the container on my lap as he left the room with Mom. I shook my head and cursed under my breath. This was ridiculous. But at this point, I had no time to waste before I had an accident, so I struggled to sit up and position myself so that I could urinate in the container. I was halfway through when the door suddenly opened and the nurse came walking in with a folder in her hand.

"What the heck," I yelled out as I pulled the robe down in a frantic motion. I quickly stopped myself before I was finished and gave her an angry, embarrassed look. Couldn't she have waited?

"It's okay, son. You can finish up. I'm just going to unhook your IV," she said casually, acting as if she saw this kind of stuff every day.

"That's all right. I was finished anyway," I said in an irritated tone as I placed the half-full container on the side of the cart and positioned myself once again on the bed, making sure I was fully covered up. "What am I doing here?" I asked, beginning to get mad that nobody had told me just yet.

"Oh, you just had a fainting spell at your school. You're just fine. Your blood pressure is normal and all of your vital signs are right on target. You can go home just as soon as the doctor signs the discharge forms."

"But why did I faint?" I asked.

"I don't know, son. You'll have to ask Dr. Sampson. I think he's talking to your parents right now."

"Well, tell Dr. whoever his name is that I want to see him, and I want to see him right now," I said firmly. By this point, I was furious that I was in the hospital. I had questions that I wanted answers to. What happened to me? Why did I go after Uncle John the way I did? Why was I here wearing a silly robe?

Later that night, Mom and Dad came up to my bedroom to check and make sure I was all right. I lifted the headphones off my ears and turned down *Smashing Pumpkins.*

"Kiddo, how are you feeling?" Dad asked as he sat down beside me.

"All right, I guess," I answered.

"Are you up to calling Uncle John right now? He wants to speak to you. He called us earlier to see how you're doing. He's very concerned about you, you know."

My stomach turned a few times. "Can't I wait until tomorrow?"

"I don't know, Matt. He's really expecting you to call tonight. It will make him happy, and he won't have to worry all night about you. How about it, pal?" Dad asked, reaching forward to tug at my basketball cap.

I nodded slowly. It was no use. "Yeah, sure. Can you hand me my phone?" I asked, too lazy to get up.

"Sure thing," Dad said, reaching to give me the phone. I waited for the two of them to leave the room before I dialed Uncle John's number. This was not going to be fun. What would he have to say to me? He was probably going to kick me off the team this time. The phone rang three times before I heard his voice.

"Hello."

"Um, hi. It's me, Matt," I said with a shaky voice.

"Hi, Matt. How are you doing?" he asked, sounding somewhat cheerful.

"I'm fine. How are you?" I asked.

"Oh, I'm doing great. Listen, about this morning, I don't know what happened between you and I, but what do you say we just put it behind us and forget it ever happened? In fact, it will be our secret. Nobody else has to know."

I hesitated for a moment. Forget about it? Make believe it never happened? Was he for real? I kicked and punched him on the bleachers in a wild fury and he was willing to just forget about it?

"Matt, are you there?" Uncle John asked, snapping me back to reality.

"Yeah, I'm here, Uncle John. Um, sure, I guess that will be fine."

"Great. Listen, Matt, I'm glad that you're okay. I really care about you, you know."

"Me too. I mean, I care about you, too. Thanks a lot," I said quietly.

"Well, I guess I'll see you on Tuesday at practice."

I nodded my head. "Yup, see you then," I said.

"Great. Goodnight, then, Matt."

"Goodnight, Uncle John," I said before cutting him off. This was totally crazy. How could he just forget about what happened this morning? I had made a complete fool out of us, and he was willing to just forget about it? I continued to stare up at my ceiling while thinking about what had happened. Something had to be wrong with me to make me act like I did this morning. It wasn't normal, that's for sure. None of the other boys had ever acted like that.

Dad opened the door and smiled as he walked in to check on me. "So, how did it go? Is everything all right between you guys?"

I nodded my head slowly. "Dad, what's my problem?" I asked in a worried tone, a few tears beginning to form in my eyes.

9

Back In Action

Things had returned back to normal the following week. Dad and I had a long discussion in my room that Saturday night about how sometimes I flew off the handle when certain things really upset me. There was nothing wrong with me, but I just reacted a little too strongly sometimes. I had promised him that I would be on my best behavior for Uncle John in the future, and that nothing similar to Saturday morning's event would ever happen again. Deep down, however, I wondered if I could safely make that promise, or would I explode at some point in the future and do something even worse? The thought really scared me, especially considering that it happened last time without me even knowing about it. It was almost like another person had stepped into my skin and took over my thoughts and actions.

The other players on the team treated me a little strangely at first, almost as if I had some sort of disease or something, but after a few days they were back to treating me like nothing had ever happened. David had been aware of the little problem I had with my temper, and acted as if it were just another day in my life. That was good, especially considering that I needed him as a friend right now more than ever. Tuesday's practice had even gone well. I didn't give Uncle John any problems whatsoever, and had even pleased him. It seemed as if both of us were trying our hardest to be on our best behavior. I performed a flawless practice and made him smile and clap for me with each drill I did. Indeed, things were returning back to the way they should have gone in the first place.

Today's practice, Thursday, went just as well. We had learned some new defensive and rebounding drills that were pretty exciting. Uncle John was teaching us the "Sky and Score" technique that proved to be an easy one for me. He lined us up on the court, seven on one side, eight on the other, as he stood at the foul line. He shot the ball, purposely hitting the rim so that it rebounded back down. The first player in line would then jump up to grab the rebound before putting it back up and hopefully sinking a basket. Each time my turn came up, I jumped as high as I could and easily sunk the ball in for two points.

"Excellent job, Matt. You're showing perfect form right there. Did everybody just see him? Matt is a good jumper, granted, but all of you can jump like that. Just catch the ball with both hands and throw it back up before you begin your descent. Keep your eye on the basket." The other boys smiled at me in admiration. I didn't want to brag, but I was the best jumper on the team. Even David had trouble getting my height, and he was almost an inch taller than I was. It's not easy being a shrimpy four feet, ten inches tall, but the right sneakers can certainly help you out.

"Okay, guys, I'd like to end the practice today by seeing some boxing out techniques. Let's do two at a time. Matt and Chris, you're up first."

Great, I thought to myself. Now I'll really shine. I could play ten times better than Chris could, and that was with both hands tied behind my back. I grabbed a ball off the rack and began to dribble towards the basket. As I got ready to shoot, Chris got in front of me and pushed in to try and block the rebound. The shot missed and bounced off the backboard as Chris held his hands high in anticipation of grabbing the shot. I tried to move around him, but he held strong, a little too strong as he pushed his butt against me.

"Hey. That was a foul," I shouted out as I let Chris grab the rebound.

Uncle John's whistle blew. *Tweet!* "He's right, Chris. You must stay right on top of the opponent, but you can't rub up against him. The idea is to try and block him with your body, but you must never intentionally bump him."

I nodded my head in agreement and took the ball from Chris. A few more drills and we had mastered it down to a science. Chris was actually a better player than

74

I gave him credit for, and I had to admit that he was trying to buddy up to me lately.

Coach blew his whistle to indicate that we were finished. "Good job, boys. Next up are Ortiz and Graham. Casey and Medeiros, I want you both to do five minutes of stretching."

I walked over to the mats at the side of the gym and began stretching with Chris.

"You're a really good player, you know," Chris said while we stretched.

I smiled at him. "Thanks, you're pretty good, too."

Chris and I had known each other from school during the past several years, but we had never spoken to one another as friends. Maybe he wasn't such a bad kid.

"I think we would make a pretty good team, you and I," Chris said.

"What do you mean?" I asked him, stretching the back of my legs until they burned.

"You know, like two on two, or something. Say, would you like to sleep over my house this weekend? We could practice in my driveway. I have a real cool hoop. It's even a ten footer."

I thought for a second. "Sure, why not. It would be fun," I said, smiling back at him.

"Great, Matt. I promise we'll have a cool time together," Chris said, returning the smile. He meant it, too. Suddenly, I could tell that there were other nice kids out there besides David. I had always been so close to him that I had ignored most everyone else, at least as far as friends went that I did stuff outside of school with. I could tell right away that Chris and I would probably become good friends.

After practice was over, Coach announced that we would have our first game next Saturday against Eastside Elementary School.

"Listen up, guys. Next Saturday, only nine days away, we have our first game over at Eastside. They're a relatively weak team, so we shouldn't have too much of a problem taking them. But just the same, we've got to be ready. We'll have a practice this Saturday from nine to twelve, then after school practices next Tuesday and Thursday. Great job today, boys."

In the locker room, Chris walked over to me on his way out. "Matt, how about if you come over my house right after practice on Saturday?"

"Sure, sounds good to me. See you later, Chris," I replied with a smile.

David gave me a strange grin. "You're going over to his house on Saturday?"

"Yeah. After we did our drill together, he asked me to sleep over. He's actually pretty cool, you know," I said, wanting David to like him, too.

"I guess so," was all David said before pulling on his sweatshirt.

I smiled at my best friend. "Yeah, but not as cool as you, Jonesy."

We slapped each other a high five. "You got that right, dude," he said with a tone of confidence.

As I walked out to the bus, I smiled to myself. So far, this week had been a great one. I was back in action on the Clarkson Challengers, my temper had been controlled with no problem, Coach was happy with my performance at the practices, and I had even made a new friend. Life was beginning to look up. Matt "Basketball" Casey was back in action.

10

My New Pal

"He goes up for the J, sinks it in for two points. The crowd goes wild 'Rah, Rah, go for it, Matt,'" I yelled as I sunk another basket in Chris's driveway.

"Awesome, dude," Chris yelled, grabbing the rebound and pushing past me to sink another two himself. "And the crowd cheers Chris 'The Man' Medeiros on as he brings his total to forty eight."

Chris returned to slap me a high five before I caught his rebound and pushed forward to perform a flawless dunk shot.

"Man, you're hot today," he yelled as we slapped each other yet another high five.

"Right on, pal," I shouted, catching the rebound and pushing forward for a set shot.

Chris intercepted it and slapped it away from me. "Oh, yeah," he said, grabbing the ball and dribbling past me with determination, laying it up for another two points. *Swoosh!* "Awesome. Fifty points for the man."

"Nice going, hot shot," I said happily.

Chris and I were getting along about as good as two boys possibly could. In fact, he was a lot of fun, and I was sorry I hadn't gotten to know him sooner.

I smiled as I watched him sink in another two pointer, catching my breath. "Nice shot, Chris."

"Thanks. Hey, are you thirsty? I am. Let's go in and get a snack."

"Sure," I agreed as Chris dropped the ball on the grass and we headed into the house.

Once inside, I was amazed at how nice their home was. The living room had all sorts of expensive leather couches and chairs with exotic paintings on the wall. Chris led me into the kitchen and opened up the refrigerator.

"Let's see. We've got Sunny D, Cherry Coke, Diet Pepsi, CranApple Juice, and, well, that's about it. What'll it be, pal?" he asked, turning to smile at me.

"Um, how about Sunny D. I love that stuff. Did you ever see that silly commercial where those guys come in from working out or something and they raid the refrigerator for the Sunny D?" I asked, chuckling at the same time.

"Yeah, that's funny," Chris said as he poured my drink, trying not to laugh. As it was, his hand was wobbling from the heavy bottle.

I grabbed the glass from him and swallowed it in one long gulp. "Playing basketball sure makes you thirsty, doesn't it?" I asked, watching him as he drank.

"Yup. Here, have some more. Hey, want some cookies?"

"Sure," I said, following him to the cookie jar beside the microwave oven. "Your house is awesome, Chris. It's nicer than mine."

"Thanks. Want to see my room now?" he asked, smiling from ear to ear.

81

"Yeah, cool."

The two of us headed up the stairs to his bedroom. Inside, I couldn't help but gaze at all of the sports stuff he had hanging on his walls.

"Wow. This is awesome," I said, smiling. "You have so much stuff in here."

"Yeah, as you can see, I love sports. I've been collecting this stuff since I was five or six. I'm really into basketball and soccer. I play soccer in the spring, and I'm also into swimming, too. Just last year, I won a medal for the boys ten-year-old division best freestyle."

"Not bad," I said, admiring his room. Chris seemed to be in seventh heaven showing off his collection to me.

"So, what's your favorite sport?" he asked, plopping down on the floor to play with his nerfball, similar to the one I had in my room.

I threw myself down next to him. "Basketball, without a doubt. I love that game like nothing else."

"Yeah, me too. It's such a cool game. I wonder why you and I were never on the same team in school. I know there's different teams and all for the lower grades, but you would think that after playing for three years, we would have gotten on the same team at one time or another."

I nodded my head at him. "Yeah, you're right. That is weird, isn't it?" We both smiled at each other.

"My favorite player is Shaq. I think he's awesome. How about you?" Chris asked, tossing his nerfball up in the air.

"Michael Jordan. Actually, I really like Kevin McHale, too. They're both so awesome," I answered, getting excited by the conversation.

"*Gross*, Casey. You're a Celtics fan? Well, they're okay, I guess," Chris said with a sarcastic tone.

"What do you mean, you guess? They rule, Medeiros," I said with authority before grabbing the nerfball from him.

"Yeah, well, nobody beats the Knicks," Chris said casually, trying to grab the ball back.

"Yeah, right. They stink, simple as that."

"Shut up, Casey, you dork," Chris said, leaning over to punch me, laughing at the same time.

I reached back over to punch him harder. "Who are you calling a dork, you geek?" I asked. Before two seconds had passed, we were rolling around on the floor, punching each other in a wild frenzy while giggling like two drunken sailors.

"Boys, what's going on in here?" Mrs. Medeiros asked, stopping beside the door.

Chris and I stopped to look up at her. "Nothing, Mom. We're just having some fun, that's all," Chris replied. We both smiled up at her and waited for her to walk away. "Hey, want to see my jersey collection?" Chris asked, jumping up to open his closet. Inside was the largest collection of basketball jerseys and tank tops imaginable to man.

"Awesome. This is so cool, dude," I said, in awe at all of the shirts. I looked through them and picked out a dark green tank top that had *Celtics* written across it. "Well, it's not Kevin's number, but it'll do for me," I said, holding it up to my chest.

"Try it on, killer," Chris said, smiling at me. I responded by pulling off my sweatshirt and sliding the tank over my head.

"It's a perfect fit," I remarked, watching him put on a red Lakers tank top with number 16 on the back. "That one's cool, too."

"For sure," Chris responded, smiling at me. "I really love red, and 16 always brings me good luck."

"You know, I have tons of these things, too. I collect them just like you do."

"Neat. Hey, you look really cool in that," Chris said.

"Thanks, dude. You know, we're going to win every game this year. You, me, and David are by far the best on the team."

"I agree with that. You know, we should do more stuff like this, I mean, get together on weekends. I'd like to do stuff with David, too," Chris said.

"Cool, we will. David's a great kid. He's funny as heck. You know, I was real mad at you when you got number 7 on the team. I wanted that number."

"So, are you still mad at me?"

"Nah, you're an okay kid," I said with a big grin on my face. "But I'm not exactly happy with number 13. That number rots, big time." Chris and I started to giggle and shake our heads. I never would have thought in a million years that I would become friends with Chris Medeiros. What a cool kid he was.

After an enjoyable dinner that evening with Chris and his parents, the two of us went up to his room to listen to his stereo.

"Pick out any CD you want," Chris said, shutting the door to his room.

I flipped through his collection and stopped at the *Goo Goo Dolls*. "Cool, let's hear this one. I love this group."

Chris came over to me and smiled, reaching for the CD. "I like them, too."

I sat down on the floor and began to toss his nerfball. Suddenly, the music blared through his stereo speakers. Chris sat down next to me and smiled as he pulled out a giant bag of Twizzlers from under his tee shirt.

I laughed out loud. "Where did you get that, dude?"

"Shh," he said, putting a finger to his lips. "I stole it from the kitchen. If my mother finds out, we're dead, so keep it quiet," Chris said, chuckling at the same time.

"Mum's the word," I replied, ripping off about five strands and shoving them into my mouth. Chris and I smiled at each other and laughed.

We spent the next couple of hours listening to his CD's, talking about all sorts of things in school from basketball, girls, teachers, and everything else that sixth graders might talk about, all the while inhaling the entire pound bag of Twizzlers.

"Oh, God, I think I'm going to puke," Chris said, frowning as he rubbed his stomach.

"Me too," I said, feeling a little sick myself. "Don't make me laugh, Chris. If you do, I'll ruin your rug."

"Geez, no joke, dude. We definitely ate too much of that stuff." Chris then flung the empty bag into the garbage. "Score. He sinks a two pointer."

I started laughing, slow at first, then harder and harder until I was forced to run down to the bathroom and throw up not only the half pound of Twizzlers I inhaled, but all of my undigested dinner as well. By the time I got back to the room, Chris was rolling around on the floor laughing like crazy.

"You'd better not be laughing at me, you dork," I said, pouncing on top of him and grabbing his head into a headlock.

"You should have seen the look on your face," Chris said as I let him up for air. "It was so funny. Man, you are too funny, Matt."

"It's the Mattster to you, Medeiros," I said proudly.

We laughed together until Chris's mother came down and told us that it was time to get ready for bed. Chris and I stopped our drunken laughter and rolled out our sleeping bags on the floor.

"I hope you don't actually have pajamas with basketballs on them," I said to Chris, half expecting him to open a drawer in his bureau and produce a set of New York Knicks pajamas.

"No, but I used to. I don't sleep in pajamas anymore. Do you?" he asked.

"Get real. We're eleven now, soon to be twelve. Pajamas are for little kids."

"Yeah, I agree," Chris replied with a smile.

We made one last trip to the bathroom before sliding into our sleeping bags for the night.

"Hey, do you know the Challengers official handshake?" Chris asked.

"What? I've never heard of it. A handshake?" I asked, completely confused.

"Yeah, it's a handshake that me and Jesse Barrett devised. It means we're all members of the Challengers. Want to learn it?"

"Sure, I guess so," I answered, not knowing what else to say.

Chris held out his hand to me. I grabbed it and let him go through the motions.

"It goes like this. You first shake like a regular handshake. That signifies your maturity, that we're sixth graders now. Then you stick your thumbs up, like this, to show that we're the best. Then you interlock your fingers like this, meaning we are inseparable members of the team." Chris and I intertwined our fingers. "Then you make a fist and bang once on top, like this, then once on the bottom, for team spirit, and you end it by giving a high five. You know what that is, obviously."

I smacked Chris's palm with my own. "Yeah, we've only been giving them to each other all day," I said, laughing a little. "Hey, that's a cool handshake. Let's do it again so I can teach it to David." We tried it again a few times until I had it down pat, then Chris smiled at me with a huge grin.

"You know, I have to say that I'm really glad I invited you over. I'm glad you're a new friend, Matt. We're pretty cool together."

"I know, dude. I'm happy we're friends, too. In fact, you're my new pal." With that said, Chris smiled and turned out the light. It had been another great day for me. I had made a new friend, one of my best ever, and the funny thing about it was that I doubted him all along, thinking he was a geek all these years. It's times like this when I learn an important lesson in life. You can never judge a book by its cover. Every person deserves a fair chance.

Andre J. Garant

11

High Scorer

"Guys, quiet down. We're just about ready to go out on the court, and I need your attention for a few minutes." We all huddled around Coach as he delivered his pep talk to us before we demolished Eastside. "Okay, I just want to let you know that today is the day we've been practicing for during the last few weeks. I know we can beat these guys cold, so let's play some ball. Are you guys psyched, or what?" he yelled.

"Yeah," we all shouted at the top of our lungs.

"The five key players know what to do. Today is your chance to show your stuff and let Eastside know that we are the best."

At long last, our first game, and I was worked up to the max. I didn't even mind wearing number 13. The uniform looked awesome on me, and on everyone else for that matter.

"All right, let's get out there and kick some butt," Coach yelled.

"Yeah," I shouted as loud as I could. My voice was barely audible over the rest of the boys. We were on fire today, simple as that.

"Good luck, Matt," Chris said to me, raising his hand for a high five.

"You too, pal," I said, smacking his palm. After we had made the rounds and wished each other luck, we strutted out onto the basketball court to field a round of cheering and applause from our spectators in the bleachers. There sure were a lot of people watching us, more than I could ever remember from our games in the fourth or fifth grade. We were now in the big league, the big time, where the action was. I took my seat in the number 4 chair, reserved for the team's Off Guard player. David was in chair number 1, a spot reserved for the Point

Guard. Chris was sitting on my left side as Big Forward, while Jesse Barrett sat to my right as Small Forward.

"Wow, look at those guys. What shrimps," I said to Chris, chuckling at the size of our opponents. Most of them were very small for sixth graders with the exception of one rather tall, clumsy looking player.

"I know," Chris said. "We'll pound them into the ground, won't we?"

"You know it," I said confidently while smiling.

When the referee blew his whistle, it was time for us to stand up and pledge allegiance to the flag. Afterwards, Coach made us take our positions on the court. I ran out with David and Chris, followed by Jesse and Jason.

"Well, this is it," I whispered to David, standing at his side.

"Yeah, I know. We can take these guys no problem," he said with a nod of the head. We both got into position as Jason walked over next to Eastside's Center in the middle jump court. The referee then walked over between them, blew his whistle, and threw the ball up in the air. Jason easily tipped the ball in David's direction, whereby David caught it and began dribbling, simultaneously making his way up the court. I weaved around the Eastside defense and positioned myself favorably near the basket. David made a perfect chest pass to Chris, who then passed it to me. I made a set shot and sunk the ball in for the first two points of the game. *Swoosh!*

"Yeah, way to go, Matt," David shouted over to me.

I smiled back briefly before following Eastside's Off Guard down the court. When he tried to pass it to one of his teammates, I intercepted it and passed it to Jesse. Jesse then brought it back down the court, passed it to Jason, who passed it to David, who followed by swooshing it in for another two points. The crowd cheered and clapped.

At half-time, we strutted back to our seats with swollen egos. So far, the score was: The Challengers, 16, Eastside, 6.

"Guys, you're doing just great out there. I like what I see as far as teamwork and passing the ball around. Jesse, I think you're lagging a little. Pick it up a bit. Matt, you're doing just fine, but try to dribble a little faster. You may get called for traveling if you don't. David, Chris, and Jason, keep up the good work. If we continue to score well, I'll send some of the other guys in for the last five minutes."

I picked up my water bottle and took a long guzzle. How could Coach say that I wasn't dribbling fast enough? I was on fire out there. In fact, eight of our sixteen points were from me, thank you very much. David had made four, Chris two, and Jason two.

When the half-time break was over, we shuffled back onto the court. Coach had instructed us to try something different. When the whistle blew again to indicate the start of play, I ran behind Jesse to fake out the Eastside Center. He started forward, eyeing the basket, but when he was ready to pass it to his Off Guard, I snuck out and intercepted it. I caught the ball easily and dribble-weaved my way back down to our side. I then passed it to

Chris, who faked a jump shot, passed it to Jason, who passed it back to David, now open, who swooshed it in for a quick two points.

"Yeah, go for the J, jerky," I yelled out to David, cheering him on. The ball rebounded and was caught by Chris who dribbled back around to the center of the court. He made believe he was going to pass to me, faked the defense out, and set the ball up for a three pointer. The ball bounced off the rim, rolled around a few times, and finally fell through.

"Awesome, Chris," I shouted, running around to cover my opponent as Eastside got the rebound and began taking the ball back down the court. They passed it back and forth a few times before finally making a shot. I jumped up and intercepted it in mid-air, slamming the ball back down and passing it to Jason, halfway down the court. He flew past his opponent while faking him out, dribbling the ball with incredible ease, and layed it up to sink yet another two points for the Challengers. *Swoosh!*

The game ended after we had scored an even thirty points, beating Eastside by a whopping eighteen points.

The scoreboard read: Home, 12, Visitor, 30. And that was even after Coach had taken David, Chris, and myself out of the game for the last few minutes, substituting us with Tony Ortiz, Paul Graham, and Derrick Raposo.

"Awesome game, guys. I'm real proud of you. You did a great job today," Uncle John said as he gave each of us a pat on the back. We then got in line to do the handshake procession, something I never really cared for. After we had ran off the court and back into the locker room, we shouted and cheered our victory as the Eastside players stuck to the other side and shook their heads at us.

"Matt, you were incredible out there. Do you realize that you scored fourteen points for us today?" Chris asked, smiling at me.

"Yes, I do, thank you," I replied, taking a bow in front of my teammates.

"So what! He still stinks at the game," David said with a sarcastic grin, punching me in the arm. We laughed together before I punched him back.

Uncle John then walked in and gave us another pep talk. "Once again, great job, guys. Today's high scorer was Matt with fourteen points, followed by David with eight points. Chris had five points, thanks to his excellent three pointer."

"Yeah, way to go, dude," I shouted, giving him a high five.

"Our next practice is on Tuesday, and we have another game next Saturday at home against Cheshire. They're a better team and we'll have to work hard to beat them."

"Just leave it to me, Coach. I'll do even better next weekend," I said, tooting my own horn.

"Great, Matt. Okay, boys, get changed up. See you Tuesday," Uncle John said before leaving us. I quickly changed out of my uniform and headed outside to meet Mom and Dad who were waiting in the bleachers, talking with David's parents. When I saw Uncle John getting ready to walk out of the gym, I called out to him.

"Uncle John, wait up."

"Yes, Matt," he said, stopping to wait for me.

I ran up to him. "So, did I do good enough today?" I asked, waiting for him to butter me up.

He chuckled briefly. "Of course you did, Matt. As long as you do your best, then you've done good enough for me."

"Yeah, but aren't you impressed with me? I got fourteen points for us today."

Uncle John smiled at me. "Yes, Matt, I'm very impressed with you. I know you're an excellent player. I have to run. Great job. See you Tuesday," he said before turning to walk down the hall.

"Yeah, see ya," I said quietly, watching him walk away. Gee whiz, I score nearly half the points for the game and all he can say is "great job, Matt?" How about something like "Matt, you are my star player and we will go down in the record books because of you", or "You did spectacularly well out there, Matt. Is there anything I can do for you to reward you for your performance? Anything at all, you just name it." Well, I guess I would have to do even better next weekend, even if it meant hogging the ball a little. I know Uncle John doesn't like it when I do that, but I could easily score twice as many points by doing it. Now that would be a way to make people bow to me. It was a risky idea, but the more I thought about it, the more I liked it.

"Matt, excellent job, pal. Are you coming home or are you going to stand there all day?" Dad asked, smiling at me from the bleachers. Apparently, I had gotten caught up in my own daydream.

"Yeah, Dad, I'm coming," I said, running over to meet him. Yup, next weekend, Matt "Basketball" Casey was going to make the headlines by scoring a record number of points for a sixth grade game. Yes, that's what I was going to do, whether Uncle John liked it or not. After all, I had a reputation and an image to protect.

12

Frustration

"So, tell me, dude, what are you planning as your strategy for the game?" I asked David as we changed in the locker room for our second game against Cheshire.

He shrugged his shoulders. "I don't know. Nothing special, I guess. How about you?"

"I'm going to sink an incredible number of points. I have to show my uncle that I can be the best player in the entire sixth grade for all schools. Yeah, the best. I just *have* to be the best," I said dreamily, staring at my gym bag with a grin on my face.

"Matt, you've gone bonkers on us again. I don't know why you always have to be the best. You're plenty good as you are. Besides, your uncle doesn't put any pressure on you, so what's the big deal?"

"The big deal is that I have to be the best, simple as that," I replied cooly, pulling on my shorts.

David shook his head at me and went back to tying his shoelaces. "You're sick, Matt, just plain sick in the head."

"You wait, David. I swear I'm going to score at least thirty points today for us."

"Whatever. I'll see you outside," he said, grabbing his water bottle and heading out the locker room door. I was one of the last to finish changing, so I hurried up a little. I guess I was too busy telling David about my plan.

Before the game was about to start, Uncle John lined us up against the far wall of the gym and told us what we had to do to win today's game.

"Listen up, you guys. Today's game will be much tougher to win than last week's. We had it made in the shade with Eastside, but Cheshire is a much stronger team all around. They've got a star defense and a Center that can knock our socks off. Let's stay focused and remember that teamwork is the name of the game. Nobody should hog the ball." With that said, Uncle John looked at me for a split second while nodding his head. I guess he was trying to tell me beforehand that he didn't want any of my fancy moves today. No such luck, I thought to myself secretly. Did he want us to win the game or not? Sure I could pass the ball to others on the team, but why take a chance on losing? "Okay, let's get out there and do our stuff. Who's the best team around?"

"We are," I shouted along with the others while stamping my feet. I really wanted to say "I am," but I knew that wouldn't go over so well with Uncle John. Lately, I was on fire, and today was only going to get better for me.

The referee blew his whistle. I walked out and took my place in between David and Chris. The ball was tossed in the air, and Jason barely tipped it in our direction. Although it was heading for Jesse, I leaped sideways and grabbed it out of his path. I then dribbled forward, maneuvering past the Cheshire defense while watching for my other teammates as open possibilities.

David was way over on the other side, and his opponent stuck to him like a bee on honey. Chris was hidden behind his opponent since he was shorter, and being that nobody was open, I threw the ball as hard as I could towards the basket and missed as it slammed off the backboard. *Bonk!*

"Matt, what was *that?*" Uncle John yelled to me with a confused look on his face. "Teamwork, Matt. Remember that."

I nodded my head and decided to ignore him. Okay, so I missed the first basket. Big deal. Next time I would get it in. The ball was now in Cheshire's hands and I raced after my opponent. When the Cheshire Big Forward saw that he was open, the ball got passed to him. I lurched forward and blocked it, simultaneously knocking my opponent to the floor. The whistle sounded.

"Foul on Clarkson number 13" the referee called out.

"Oh, man," I said. I looked over and saw Uncle John shake his head.

My opponent from Cheshire went to the foul line and easily sunk two baskets. Now I was starting to get mad, but I had to keep my cool. The ball came back in our direction and I ran full speed ahead to get into an open position. David had it now as he dribbled forward towards me. He scanned his path, saw that Chris and I were both relatively open, and passed it to Chris. Chris looked up, saw that I was not in a good area, and took the shot himself. *Swoosh,* the ball sounded as it sailed through the net.

"Great shot, Chris," Uncle John yelled as we got our first two points, the game now tied.

"Chris, I was open, you know," I shouted over to him angrily.

"I looked for you, but you weren't paying attention," he said back. I shook my head and cursed under my breath.

Coach saw me and shook a finger. "Matt, keep your eyes and ears open. Pay attention now," he shouted.

"What?" I yelled back, flashing an angry look his way. What on earth was he talking about? I *was* paying attention, all the time for that matter.

Cheshire went up for a set shot, sunk it in for two, and the ball rebounded in my direction. I grabbed it and tore off down the court, dribbling as fast as I could. I swung around their defense, looked at who was open on my team, but decided to take a shot at it myself, something we were told never to do. You were always supposed to pass the ball at least once. I sunk it in for two.

"Matt, come on. You're supposed to pass the ball. I don't want to see that again," Uncle John yelled out to me.

"Come on, Matt. Nice shot, but I was open, you know," David yelled to me.

"I know," was all I said as I heard the crowd cheering in my own mind. I was getting back in action.

At half-time, the score was: Cheshire, 14, Clarkson, 10. I took my seat and wiped my forehead with a dry towel. I sure was working up a sweat today.

"Guys, the defense factor is lacking today. I also don't see a good amount of teamwork. Matt, you especially need to pass the ball more. Even if you know for sure that you can make the shot, pass it to someone. I really want that ball passed two and three times before someone shoots. I know you guys can do better right now, so let's do it," Coach instructed, pacing back and forth in front of us.

I smiled and thought of how I would take the second half of the game. When the whistle blew, I ran out and got into position. When the ball came my way, I stole it away from Jesse and turned to run down the court. Chris and David were right beside me, but when I saw that they were being covered too closely, I stopped short and made a flawless set shot to sink it in for two.

"Matt, come on," Chris shouted to me. "What are you doing?"

Coach walked out to the court and yelled at me. "I told you not to do that. If I see it again, I'm taking you out for the rest of the game." I tried my hardest to keep my mouth shut. I wanted to tell him off right now so badly, but I knew I had to keep my cool. Here I was scoring baskets for our team and I was getting yelled at. The pressure mounted as the second half wore on, but David and Chris were scoring nicely, and by the time there was only a minute and a half left on the clock, the score was tied at 18-18. I was trying my hardest to pass the ball around, and was doing a little better, but the pressure was too much for us now. I had to take matters back into my own hands.

Uncle John blew his whistle to call time out. We walked over to form a huddle near him.

"All right, we can't screw this up now. I want the five starting players to listen closely. Cheshire has the ball right now. Keep the defense strong, and when the ball is back in our hands, then I want to see Chris, David, and Matt perform the Clarkson Express. Now is the time for it. Do you guys understand?"

We all nodded our heads. The Clarkson Express was a technique we had learned in practice whereby we got a rebound and passed the ball back and forth among David, Chris, and I until we were back at our end of the court. Whoever had the ball would fake a set shot, then pass it back to one of the others, whoever was open, fake another set, and pass it to the third. That person then faked it once more quickly before setting it up for the final shot. We had it down to a science by now.

"Matt, you know what to do, right?" David asked, giving me a serious look as we got back out to the court.

I nodded quickly. "Of course I do, Jonesy."

Cheshire weaved their way down the court, aiming to win the game with a narrow margin. Their defense was too strong for us and they ended up scoring another basket with only 48 seconds left to play. They were up by one basket. Chris jumped up to catch the rebound, barely got it, and threw it back to David who dribbled down the court. When he got to the far end, he passed it to Chris once again. Chris faked a set shot and threw the ball to me. I caught it no problem. Now the pressure was on and I could feel the sweat pouring down my face and chest. I could lay it up and win the game for us, or I could do what Coach said and fake it before passing it back to David. Decisions, decisions. I hated them.

"Come on, Matt" Uncle John yelled to me along with my other teammates on the bench. The clock had 32 seconds left. I looked at David, then at the basket, and back to David before deciding to take my chances and shoot it. I didn't even fake it, but lobbed it up with a spin that took it straight for the rim. I could hear Coach yelling at me along with Chris and David. The ball bounced off the rim and down into the hands of the Cheshire Center, easily the tallest boy on the court. He graciously weaved the ball back down the court before passing it to the Cheshire Off Guard who layed it up just in time to score two points as the buzzer went off.

I dropped down in a hunch, my head between my legs. "You blew it, Matt," I whispered to myself. The Cheshire boys were cheering and yelling like mad, but nobody on my team said a word. By the time I looked up, Chris, David, Jason, and Jesse had strolled off the court, shaking their heads in disbelief. I felt about as big as an ant on a football field. I stood still and watched Uncle John look out at me before shaking his head and quickly turning back around.

Finally, I got up the strength and courage to walk back to my seat and face the music. Nobody said a word to me as I wiped my forehead with my towel.

"Guys, you gave it your all today, and I can only look favorably on that. They were just a strong team, that's all. Good job. Let's shake hands with them and get changed up." I stood up and got into line to slap high fives with the members of the Cheshire team, all of whom had huge smiles on their faces. Sure, why not? They had just won the game by a lucky basket, thanks to my dumb mistake. When we were finished, I strolled back to my seat with the others and grabbed my towel and water bottle. I was just about to head to the locker room behind David and Chris when Coach spoke out.

"Matthew, please stay for a minute."

I turned around and sat back in my seat with a sheepish grin, waiting for the worst. I knew he was furious with me, especially since he called me by my full name.

"All I can say is that I am extremely disappointed in you. I know you want to win, Matt, but so does everybody else. You have got to stop this selfish behavior on the court. You were supposed to pass the ball to David and *he* was supposed to lay it up, not you. We have gone through this drill time and time again. What's the matter with you? Do you not understand it yet? Did you not know what to do out there?"

I shot him an angry look. "I wanted to win, that's all," I shouted to him, my anger rising like a spring flood within me. "Is that okay with you, that I wanted to win? Do I need your permission every single time I want to make a shot? Well, do I?" I blurted out, not even giving him a chance to speak.

"Matt, that is not the issue here and you...."

"What, I can't take a shot when I know I can get it in? You know something, Uncle John, if I can't play the game by *my* rules, then I won't be on your stupid team at all. You'll lose every single game without me."

"Matthew, stop it right..."

"No, *you* stop it," I hollered back. "You can't coach for beans, you know that?" By now, my voice was so loud that Mom and Dad had walked over to see what was the matter. A few other spectators were curiously listening in.

"Matthew," Dad said to me while putting a firm hand on my shoulder. "Is there a problem here?"

"Yeah, *him*," I yelled, pointing a finger right in Uncle John's face. "He's yelling at me because I took a shot when I was supposed to pass the stupid ball."

"Matthew, I never yelled at you. I just want you to understand how important teamwork is when playing this game. You can't hog the ball like you did. You should have passed it over to David. You have got to learn good sportsmanship," Uncle John said, trying to calm me down.

"Yeah, whatever," I said loudly, getting up from my seat despite Dad's hand on my shoulder. I stormed away from them and ran for the locker room.

"Matthew, you come back here right now," Dad shouted to me.

I ignored him and continued to run for the locker room.

"Matt, come on back. Let's talk about this," Uncle John called out when I was just about in the locker room.

"Shut up," I muttered under my breath as I walked into the locker room, practically knocking Chris and Jason over in the process.

"Hey, Matt. Are you all right? It's just a game, you know. It's not the end of the world," Chris said to me, standing by his locker while changing into his regular clothes.

"Just leave me alone," I mumbled, fumbling to open my locker.

David stopped beside me on his way out. "Matt, don't make such..."

"*Go,*" I yelled, cutting him off in mid-sentence. David simply shook his head at me and walked out of the locker room. I sat down, hung my head between my knees and let the first few tears escape my eyes.

13

It's My Way

"Matthew, hurry up. Uncle John is on his way over to pick you up," Mom called up the stairs to me.

"I'm hurrying as fast as I can, Mom, and stop calling me Matthew. Can't you just say Matt, please?" I yelled back, combing my hair in front of the bathroom mirror.

"Matthew, I mean, Matt, honestly, dear," she said at the bottom of the stairs. I shook my head at her response and gave myself a final inspection. It was Sunday, the day after that terrible basketball game against Cheshire, and I was not in a good mood, and that was putting it mildly. I figured I looked decent enough to go out for lunch with Uncle John, wearing faded blue jeans a

117

few sizes too big for me, a grungy sweatshirt, an old pair of hi-tops which were about ready to be put out of their misery, and of course my favorite Celtics cap. Besides, I certainly didn't need to impress Uncle John with my appearance. Lately, it seemed that he wasn't impressed with anything I did, on or off the court.

A horn sounded from the front driveway.

"Matt, that must be him. Are you ready?" Mom called up the stairs.

"Yes, yes, yes, already. I'm coming. Just hold your horses," I answered impatiently before coming out of the bathroom and bounding down the stairs two at a time.

"Honey, you're getting a little old to be doing that now, don't you think?" Mom asked with a tired tone in her voice when I landed with a loud thump on the floor.

"No," was all I said before letting her peck me on the cheek. "Come on, Mom. Let me go," I said, getting mad at her when she tried to kiss me a second time.

"Oh, all right, Mr. Bad Mood. My baby is growing up too fast," she said as I opened the front door.

"Mom, I'm not your baby anymore, and I'm not growing up too fast. In fact, I'm growing up too *slow*," I said before stepping out onto the front porch. I thought I heard a groan from her just before I slammed the door shut. I wished I could just turn the clock ahead about five or six years. That way I could get my license, have Dad buy me a car, and start driving to school. It would also mean more freedom. No more angry talks from Uncle John. I tried to form a weak smile as I approached his car at the top of the driveway. I could hardly wait to hear what he had to say to me at lunch. Let me guess, he was probably going to kick me off the team, right?

"Hi, Matt. How's it going today?" he asked when I opened the car door and plopped down in the front seat.

"Just fantastic," I replied sarcastically, pulling my seat belt on.

"So, where do you feel like eating today?" he asked, now backing the car out onto the street.

"I don't care. You pick the place," I replied without looking at him.

"Well then, how about Spanky's? They have great pizza."

"Sure, I guess," I said. Spanky's was a new restaurant in town that did indeed have good pizza and burgers, not to mention their buffalo wings. Although I was happy with Uncle John's choice, I sure wasn't going to give in and pretend that everything was fine. The ride to Spanky's was anything but fun. I stared out the window and tried to count how many houses we had passed. For some reason, I just couldn't act myself anymore, the way I used to act around Uncle John, all happy and smiley. Lately, I was bummed out, and it was always about the stupid Clarkson Challengers.

Uncle John finally broke the silence. "You know, Matt, we have to get over this tension between us. I'm doing my best to treat you fairly, but you don't seem to want to give me a chance. We have to talk about this today and get it resolved once and for all so that we can go on with the team. Your behavior is not only affecting me, but also the other boys."

I pretended to ignore him and continued to count houses. Forty three, forty four, forty...

"Matt, did you just hear me? Please don't ignore me. This is very hard for me to talk to you like this. We've always been the best of friends, best pals. What's wrong, kiddo? Please don't shut me out."

"I'll talk to you when we get to the restaurant," I said rudely, my face still turned to look out the window.

When we finally got to Spanky's, the two of us sat down in a booth near the window. I flung my jacket against the wall and grabbed a menu, wanting to do anything to keep my attention off Uncle John. I noticed him looking at me, but I pretended to ignore him.

"Matt, please, can we talk now?"

"There's really nothing to talk about, unless of course you're willing to let me play by my rules. Didn't you hear what I said to you yesterday?" I asked, still looking down at the menu.

"What, you mean about letting you play your own way?" he asked, laughing a little.

"Yeah, that's exactly what I mean," I shot back, now looking up at him with angry eyes. I was mad at him for making a joke out of it.

The waitress walked over to take our order. Uncle John smiled at her while I sunk my head down and began to pout all over again.

"Hi, we'll have a large pizza with the works along with an order of buffalo wings. For drinks, I'll have a large coffee. What do you want to drink, Matt?" Uncle John asked.

"A Coke," I answered flatly, sticking the menu back in the holder near the salt and pepper shakers.

"Matt, listen, I can't let you play by your own rules. That's why I am the coach and you're not. If all the other boys wanted to play by their own rules, then we wouldn't have a team. We'd have complete chaos and everybody would be running around without a clue as to what they should be doing. Have you ever heard of anyone on another team playing without rules from the coach?" Uncle John asked.

"Yeah, I have," I lied to him. It was worth a shot.

"Oh, really? When and where?"

"I don't remember, but it was last year when I was on the fifth grade team. One of the kids could do whatever he wanted since he was the best player. The coach didn't care what he did. He was never yelled at for making a basket, I'll tell you that."

"Matt, that's complete nonsense. I know you know better than that. You mean to tell me there was a kid on the team who was better than you?" he asked, teasing me now to try and snap me out of my foul mood.

"No, he was on a team from another school," I said, not giving in an inch. So what if my story was all made up? It sounded good.

"Come on, now. You're making this all up. I realize that you want to call the shots here, but I can't let you do that. I'm the coach for the team. I make the rules, and I give the orders..."

"Or else what?" I asked, catching him off guard.

Uncle John thought for a minute. "Well, I guess I'd have to ask you to leave the team, but I know you don't want..."

"Yes, I *do* want that. Listen to me, Uncle John. Either I play by my own rules or I don't play at all. Do you hear me now? It's my way or no way," I said, my voice rising along with my temper once again.

Uncle John shook his head at me. "Matthew, listen to me. You have to stop this silly behavior. I've never seen you act so stubborn in all my life. What happened to the sweet boy I've always known?"

"He's gone. This is the new Matt Casey. It's Matt "Basketball" Casey, and I am no longer a sweet little boy. I'm almost twelve years old and I expect to be treated like an adult," I said, my voice carrying over to the nearby tables.

"Well, then, I'm sorry, Matt "Basketball" Casey, but until you can act like an adult, you will not be treated like one," Uncle John said through gritted teeth while leaning across the table at me.

I pushed my back up against the booth. "Fine, I quit your stupid team. You can take the Clarkson Challengers and stick them up your butt," I said angrily, grabbing my jacket and making a mad dash for the door.

Uncle John got up to follow me. "Matt, just where do you think you're going? Come back and eat some pizza." He caught up to me just in time and yanked my sweatshirt as I tried to squeeze through the door.

"Leave me alone. I hate you," I yelled out.

"Matt, please. Everyone is staring at us," Uncle John whispered to me as I let him lead me back to the table.

"Who cares?" I said softly, my voice shaking as I tried to hold back the tears. I dropped back down into the booth where I covered my face with my hands and started to cry.

Andre J. Garant

14

Outside Help

Mom and Dad had decided that I definitely needed to make a visit to see Dr. Liebowitz about my problems with Uncle John and the Clarkson Challengers. Things had not gone all that well at Spanky's on Sunday, and Uncle John took me home with swollen eyes and an empty stomach. I was too upset to eat, and just wanted to get back to my room to listen to some music. Before he dropped me off, however, we had agreed that I would leave my position as Off Guard for the Challengers. It was decided that Nathan Pixley would fill the spot since he was number 16 on Coach's list of players, the next person to join the team if someone had to leave.

Not only was it bad enough that I was off the team and that I had to see Dr. Liebowitz for an undetermined number of sessions, but Uncle John was going to attend the meetings as well. I was not overly thrilled about that, but Mom and Dad had told me it was for the best for us to work things out together so there would be no hard feelings between us.

When Mom had dropped me off at Dr. Liebowitz's office the following Wednesday after school, Uncle John was already there, talking quietly with him.

I opened the door to the office and walked in.

"Matthew, how nice to see you again. Please, have a seat right here," Dr. Liebowitz said, motioning for me to sit next to Uncle John. He held out his hand to me.

I shook it, frowning at the fact that it felt like a cold fish. "Hi, Dr. Liebowitz."

"Matthew, let's get started right away. As you know, we are on limited time here, and I can sense that we have a lot to talk about."

"Fine," I said, nodding my head weakly.

"Why don't you tell us how you're feeling right now."

"Fine, I guess," I said, shrugging my shoulders, not knowing what else to say. Should I tell him that I felt like a pile of dog poop?

"It's okay, Matthew. Please be open with us. We need to know. How are you really feeling?" Dr. Liebowitz asked.

I looked down at the floor and figured I should just be honest with him. "Like garbage, actually," was my response.

"Good, good. Now we're getting somewhere. Why do you feel like garbage?"

"Well for starters, I'm off the team, I have no life anymore, and people think I'm a loser. Does that answer your question?" I asked, looking up at him with a sarcastic grin.

"Matthew, why do you think that you're off the team? Tell me about it."

"I don't know. Why not ask *him*," I said, jerking my thumb in Uncle John's direction.

"I want to hear your side of the story first, Matthew."

"Dr. Liebowitz, it's Matt, not Matthew. I hate it when people call me that."

"Sure, Matt. That's fine. Please, answer the question."

"Um, I don't really know. He got all mad at me because he thought I was hogging the ball from my teammates. I was just trying to win the game for us, and just before the end of the game, it was a tiebreaker, and I thought I could make the shot, so I took it. That's when he blew up at me."

"I see, Matthew, I mean, Matt. And how did he blow up at you?"

Uncle John was now looking at me intently.

"He just gave me a dirty look and then shook his head at me. I felt bad enough as it was. I missed the shot and everybody was mad at me. That's about it."

"Matt, did your uncle speak to you about the fact that he didn't want you to hog the ball beforehand, say, in earlier practices and games?" Dr. Liebowitz asked.

I blushed as I felt my face get hotter. "Um, well, yeah, I guess so."

"Specifically, do you remember what he said to you?"

I looked down at my sneakers and thought for a second. "It was something like we shouldn't hog the ball, and that we had to pass it at least two or three times first before making a shot. It had something to do with being good sports, or sportsmanship, something like that."

"And did you not follow his directions during the last game when he asked you not to hog the ball?"

"No, I followed his directions," I said in my own defense, but lying to him at the same time.

"How so?" Dr. Liebowitz inquired with a curious look on his face.

"I didn't hog the ball at all. I just took shots when I knew I could make them, except I missed the last shot which cost us the game."

"Matthew, I'm sorry, Matt, your uncle tells me that you did hog the ball, and that that was the sole reason why he was upset with you. He said that you were disobeying him on purpose, or so it seemed."

"That's a load of bull," I shouted, flashing an angry look at Uncle John who simply shook his head and looked away.

"Matt, please. Let's calm down. It seems that part of this problem stems from your temper. Why do you get so upset at your uncle? Can you tell me what happened between you two a few weeks ago in the school bleachers?" Dr. Liebowitz asked.

"That was supposed to be between us. And you said you would forget about it, Uncle John. What, did you lie to me? You're a jerk, you know," I said angrily.

"Matt, calm down," Dr. Liebowitz urged. "Let's talk about this openly. We can't keep any secrets if we are to gain anything from our sessions. Please tell me what happened on that day. I want to hear your side of the story."

I shook my head. "This is so stupid. I don't know how it all started. I guess I wanted to be Point Guard, and my friend David got it. Then I was mad because Chris

Medeiros got Big Forward, and I felt he stunk at the game. But I don't mind that now. Chris and I are friends, and he's actually a pretty good player. But I was really mad because Uncle John gave me number 13, a bad luck number," I said, nodding my head in my uncle's direction. "I told him I wanted number 7 since it always brings me good luck. So, what does he do? He gives me number 13."

"Matthew, is it true that you stormed off the court and went up to the bleachers?"

"Yeah. He told me to. He said that I was disobeying him or making rude remarks. I don't know what his problem was that day," I said, now getting completely upset with the direction this session was heading in.

"*My* problem? This is not about me, Matt," Uncle John said.

"John, please. Let's let Matt do the talking right now," Dr. Liebowitz said firmly.

"The only problem I have is *you*," I shouted, looking directly at Uncle John.

"Matthew, please," Dr. Liebowitz said.

"It's Matt, already. Gee whiz, get it right."

"I'm sorry. Matt, please tell me what you said to your uncle that made him send you up to the bleachers to sit out the practice that morning."

"I don't remember. It was like three weeks ago. I can't remember everything, you know."

"Please try, Matt," Dr. Liebowitz urged.

I shook my head. "Geez, I don't know. I said something about Chris, like he couldn't play to save his life, and why did he get number 7. Then Uncle John told me to stop talking, and that I was interrupting him or something dumb like that. So I kind of argued with him in front of everyone and he told me that I should sit out the practice. I wasn't even doing anything wrong, for God sakes."

"Then what happened?"

"What do you mean? I went up and sat on the bleachers, what else?

"And did your uncle come up to talk to you when the other players started practicing?"

"Yeah," I said, looking down at the floor.

"And what did he say?"

"Look, can we end right here? I'm getting tired of this. It sucks," I said firmly, squirming in my seat.

"Please, Matt. We're almost done. Just answer a few more questions for me, okay?"

I looked down at my sneakers and slouched a little lower in my seat. "He tried to talk to me, something about that I wasn't acting like myself, and he wanted to know what was wrong with me. He then told me that I would have to change my behavior if I wanted to stay on the team or else he was going to suspend me."

"What happened after he told you that?"

I was beginning to get very hot under my shirt, and my face was turning redder by the minute. "I told him that he didn't care about me, something like that."

"And then what happened, Matt?" Dr. Liebowitz asked, the tension in the room mounting like crazy. I wanted to jump out of my seat and run out the door, to do anything to get out of the office.

"I, um, kicked him, I think."

"Matt, is it true that you began a violent temper tantrum on your uncle and beat him up in front of your teammates?"

"Yeah, but only because he made me really angry. It's not like I'm happy about it or anything like that. Besides, this was supposed to be our secret, and I did apologize to him the next day on the phone."

"Matt, what do you think caused you to react like that to your uncle? It's certainly not the normal behavior an eleven-year-old would exhibit."

I looked down at my sneakers again, turning my face away from the two of them. "I don't know," I said weakly, my eyes filling up with tears. "I guess I have something wrong with me, don't I?" I managed to ask, just before my eyes released a floodgate of tears.

Uncle John stood up and came over to me. "Matt, it's okay to cry. You're going to be just fine. Just let it all out now."

Dr. Liebowitz got up and walked over to the other side of my chair, handing me a wad of tissues. "Matt, this is good for you to do. We're going to help you out. We'll fix whatever is wrong with you. Just keep crying," he said, patting my shoulder. I kept crying and crying, right up until Mom had arrived to pick me up. Dr. Liebowitz made her wait outside until he had finished up the session. When I had finally dried my eyes and regained my composure, he told me when the next meeting would be.

"Matt, our next session will be a week from today, at the same time. You did extremely well today, and I think we made some big progress here," he said while smiling at me. For some reason, I did feel better about things, almost as if a giant weight had been lifted from my back. On my way out the door, I smiled at Uncle John and said goodbye to him.

"Goodbye, Uncle John."

Not only was *I* surprised by this, but he almost fell over from shock. He simply nodded his head at me and tried to say something, but he didn't. Who knows, maybe things really would get better for us.

Andre J. Garant

15

A Lesson In Life

"Pick out anything you want, pal," Uncle John said to me as we made our way down the buffet at Ponderosa. "Go ahead, pile it on. Don't be bashful."

I looked up and smiled at him. "You'll be sorry, dude."

It was nearly a month after our first meeting with Dr. Liebowitz, and after two more sessions, we had worked everything out between us. I was no longer mad at Uncle John, and was finally able to act my old self again. We had decided, however, that I would remain off the Challengers for the rest of the season, but I didn't feel so bad when Uncle John appointed me to be his official team manager. I felt important now that I could carry around a black book that kept all of his important information as well as our team schedule for the rest of the year. Life wasn't so bad after all, and the rest of the boys on the team weren't mad at me anymore, either. Things were basically returning back to normal once again, and not a moment too soon.

"That's it for me, Uncle John," I said triumphantly, piling two biscuits on top of my already heaping plate. I wasn't sure if I would be able to eat all of it, but what the heck. I didn't get taken out to eat all the time, so why not pig out and enjoy it? The two of us sat down at a table in the corner.

"So, do you think we'll beat the Lasers today?" I asked before shoving a buttered biscuit in my mouth.

"Well, I think we have a good chance. I don't want to be overly optimistic, though. We've lost you on the team, and Nathan just doesn't cut the mustard," Uncle John answered, smiling at me.

"Let's face it, Uncle John," I said, talking a mile a minute with my mouth overflowing with food. "Nobody can replace me. I'm what they call 'Indisposable.'"

Uncle John laughed out loud. "Matt, I think you mean 'Indispensable.'"

I nodded my head. "Whatever. I'm good. Let's just leave it at that."

He took a bite of his chicken. "Well, I won't argue with that, and I certainly do miss having you on the court, but I really can use you on the sidelines. In fact, I'd be lost without you as my official manager."

"Yeah, I kind of like it, too," I agreed, dropping a mass of mashed potatoes with gravy all over my new L.A. Lakers tee shirt. "Shoot, look what I just did," I said, giggling at the same time. "What a dork I am sometimes."

Uncle John laughed again. "Well, I can see where you got your table manners from. Your father and I were always the pigs at the dinner table."

"Were you really?" I asked, trying to wipe as much of the potatoes off my shirt as I could.

"Honestly. We were always getting into trouble like that."

"Oh, man. You're funny sometimes," I said, forming a huge smile.

"You're the funny one, kiddo," Uncle John said, leaning forward and pulling my Celtics cap down over my eyes.

"Hey, I can't see, you bozo," I yelled out, grabbing his arm to make him stop. We both laughed out loud until our stomachs hurt.

Later on at the game, it was half-time, and we were ahead by six points. The Lasers certainly were good, but the Challengers were on fire today. David had scored twelve points already, and Chris was close behind with eight.

Uncle John called everyone over into a huddle. "Okay, guys, let's keep up the defense. Don't let them take it away from us. Chris, you are showing excellent form today, and David, well, just keep up the good work. The rest of you guys need to hustle a little more. Let's keep it going. Let me hear who's the best team," he said loudly.

"We are," I yelled as loud as I could with my teammates, giving each of them a high five. When the whistle blew to end half-time, I took my seat next to

Raymond and kept a close eye on the game. If we won today, we would have a record of 4-2, not too bad considering I was no longer on the team. But, to be honest with you, my feelings had changed about myself. I was no longer the selfish brat I used to be, always thinking I was ten times better than everyone else. Sure, I was good, but so were the other guys. My attitude, for one, was much better. I didn't cry anymore like a baby when things didn't go my way, or when somebody told me something I didn't like. I learned to take the good with the bad, and I made a vow that I would never, ever, under any circumstances, raise my voice to Uncle John the way I did a few months ago. He was being very nice to me, and we were getting along great lately.

David and Chris were back to being my best pals, and we got together at least once a week to have some fun. Even David had become good friends with Chris, and the two of them were practically inseparable these days. I don't really know what made me change so much during the last month, but stupid things didn't bother me anymore. If I had a bad day and things didn't go my way, then so what? Tomorrow would be another day. Life was too much fun to worry about being number 1 on the team, or making more baskets than anybody else. And my bad temper had even gone away completely, and now my biggest problem was not being able to control my incredible laughing fits. Sometimes I would giggle myself to death at school or when I played basketball with Uncle John in the driveway. It was almost as if I was on laughing gas or something. You want to know something else? I don't mind being called Matthew anymore. It used to make my skin crawl, but now people can call me anything they want. Matthew, Matt, Dork, Slimeface, it doesn't matter to me. The Mattster is still in, however.

When the final buzzer rang, the Challengers had defeated the Lasers 24-20, a close victory, but a good one. I ran out to join in the tremendous energy of hugging, high fives, and pats on the back.

"Yeah, we won guys. Nice going. Great game," I shouted. It had turned out to be one of our more exciting games, and I wasn't bothered one bit by the fact that I wasn't out on the court scoring points. What became important to me was that I was there with my teammates, cheering them on every step of the way.

The following morning was Sunday, and the weather was too nice to stay inside. After pulling on my sweats and an old pair of hi-tops, I ran outside to shoot some baskets. Although it was only March, warmer weather was making its first appearance, and the birds were beginning to chirp in the trees around the house. The air smelled fresh and clean, and I took a deep breath before taking my first shot.

Suddenly, a horn sounded from a car on the street, and I noticed that it was Uncle John. I waved and smiled to him.

"Mind if I shoot a few with you?" he asked as he got out of the car.

"Sure. I could go for some practice. I'm a little rusty, you know, not having played in a while," I said, dribbling the ball in front of him.

"I hear you, pal," he said, getting into position.

I got into my ready stance, gauged my distance from the basket, then pushed forward, dribbling the ball with gusto while weaving around Uncle John. When I got to within a close shooting distance, I faked a lay up, then quickly passed the ball over to him with a powerful chest pass. Uncle John was not prepared, and the ball slammed off his stomach.

"Wow, Matt. I thought you were going to shoot it," he said, completely taken by surprise.

I laughed. "So did I."

He hesitated for a moment after picking up the ball. "So how come you didn't? You had a perfect shot right there."

"Hey, I did learn a thing or two from you this year, you know," I said happily.

Uncle John smiled and laughed. He then walked up to me and put his arm around my shoulder to pull me tight against him. "You know something. I think I really like the new Matt Casey."

"Yeah, me too."

Summary

I'm Gonna Win features Matt Casey as an eleven-year-old basketball all-star. Now in the sixth grade, Matt finally gets to play in the big leagues, the Clarkson Senior League Team. Matt's greatest ambition is to be Point Guard and sink more baskets than any other player in the school's history. Since his Uncle John is the coach of the Senior League, Matt figures he will be guaranteed to receive special treatment. There's only one problem, however, and that's Matt's terrible temper when things don't go his way.